Do I *Even* Matter?

SOFIA GRACE

WESTBOW
PRESS®
A DIVISION OF THOMAS NELSON
& ZONDERVAN

WestBow Press books may be ordered through booksellers or by contacting:

WestBow Press
A Division of Thomas Nelson & Zondervan
1663 Liberty Drive
Bloomington, IN 47403
www.westbowpress.com
844-714-3454

Because of the dynamic nature of the Internet, any web addresses or
links contained in this book may have changed since publication and
may no longer be valid. The views expressed in this work are solely those
of the author and do not necessarily reflect the views of the publisher,
and the publisher hereby disclaims any responsibility for them.

Any people depicted in stock imagery provided by Getty Images are
models, and such images are being used for illustrative purposes only.
Certain stock imagery © Getty Images.

ISBN: 978-1-6642-1686-0 (sc)
ISBN: 978-1-6642-1687-7 (hc)
ISBN: 978-1-6642-1685-3 (e)

Library of Congress Control Number: 2020925389

Print information available on the last page.

WestBow Press rev. date: 01/30/2021

Presented to:

From:

Date:

To God, thank you for giving me the strength and wisdom to write a book—something I never thought I could do.

To my dad, thank you for your unconditional love. May you rest in peace, Daddy. You'll always be in my heart.

Contents

Appendices

Psalm 38

LORD, do not rebuke me in your anger or discipline me in your wrath.

Your arrows have pierced me, and your hand has come down on me.

Because of your wrath there is no health in my body; there is no soundness in my bones because of my sin.

My guilt has overwhelmed me like a burden too heavy to bear.

My wounds fester and are loathsome because of my sinful folly.

I am bowed down and brought very low; all day long I go about mourning.

My back is filled with searing pain; there is no health in my body.

I am feeble and utterly crushed; I groan in anguish of heart.

All my longings lie open before you, Lord; my sighing is not hidden from you.

My heart pounds, my strength fails me; even the light has gone from my eyes.

My friends and companions avoid me because of my wounds; my neighbors stay far away.

Those who want to kill me set their traps, those who would harm me talk of my ruin; all day long they scheme and lie.

I am like the deaf, who cannot hear, like the mute, who cannot speak.

I have become like one who does not hear, whose mouth can offer no reply.

LORD, I wait for you; you will answer, Lord my God.

For I said, "Do not let them gloat or exalt themselves over me when my feet slip."

For I am about to fall, and my pain is ever with me.

I confess my iniquity; I am troubled by my sin.

Many have become my enemies without cause; those who hate me without reason are numerous.

Those who repay my good with evil lodge accusations against me, though I seek only to do what is good.

LORD, do not forsake me; do not be far from me, my God.

Come quickly to help me, my Lord and my Savior.

Introduction

Challenges Build Character

The Lord upholds all those who are falling and
raises up all those who are bowed down.
—Psalm 145:14

Falling

Have you ever felt like you were falling? Have you ever felt like no
one was listening and no one cared? Have you ever felt that living
was so unbearable that the only way to stop the pain was to end your
life? Maybe you are feeling this right now.

Years before I accepted Jesus as my Savior, I experienced the
most painful, difficult, and darkest time of my life. Things were so
unbearable that it took every ounce of energy I had just to survive. I
became severely depressed, fell, and hit rock bottom. I attempted to
commit suicide, and I ended up strapped down in the psychiatric unit.

Raises Up

God can raise us up without us even realizing it is happening. God
started to raise me up while I was still a patient at the hospital.
Ironically, I was leading a "life-changing session." Shortly after
returning home, the Holy Spirit led me to a Christian church, which

ignited a passion in me to have a relationship with God, study His Word, and share it with others. God had a plan for me, and He has a plan for you too. God raised me up, and He put it in my heart to write this book and share what I have learned.

This book is about my testimony as well as the testimony of others who have fallen through affairs, addiction, divorces, financial difficulties, loss of loved ones, being orphaned, and suicide. It also includes beautiful stories of being raised up through family reunions, marriage resolutions, recovery from addictions, and discovering newfound strengths by having a relationship with God. We want to share with you our stories of God's goodness and faithfulness.

God touched your heart today. There is a story written here that He wants you to read, and I pray that you will give it a try. God is lovingly waiting to hear back from you.

CHAPTER 1

Why Me God?

"For I know the thoughts and plans that
I have for you," says the Lord.
—Jeremiah 29:11 (AMP)

Thoughts and Plans

Have your plans in the past worked? What are your plans and dreams for the future?

New Year's Day is my favorite holiday. It is an "official" day of new everything. Many people come up with New Year's resolutions, and for many years, my resolution was to diet and exercise, but it never really worked. I especially enjoy this holiday because it provides me an opportunity to get even more organized, clean everything in my house, plan for the year, and reset. It is an opportunity for a new beginning.

My 2020 New Year's resolution was different. It was not about me; it was all about God. By putting God first in my life—and with His help—my resolution is first and foremost to become a better person than I was last year with the goal of glorifying God by finishing this book. That was it. No other thoughts or plans. Why not?

For many years, my thoughts and plans were all about me. I

wanted to make sure I moved up in my career, provided financially for my family, was a good mom and wife, and was healthy. While these are good thoughts and plans, it never included what I could do for God. I was not good about putting God first in my life until He sent me His first message, and it changed my life forever.

God's First Message to Me

It was a cold, quiet, and beautiful Saturday morning in November 2013. The sun was shining, the leaves from the trees had fallen, and I was looking out the upstairs window. With a smile on my face, I successfully finished reading my very first book of the Bible. It was the book of Matthew, the first of sixty-six books in the Bible. I did not just read it; I studied it and highlighted the lines that seemed important or worth memorizing—just like an old college textbook. It was a practice that I was very familiar with. My husband calls me a "terminal student," and he is right because I love studying.

Suddenly, the most amazing thought came—and I found myself responding to someone. I was unsure about what or who I was communicating with. It felt different, extraordinary, and confusing. The force felt a little stronger, and when another thought came, I realized it was God. He communicated to me through His Spirit. It was not an audible voice; He spoke in my heart. It was an incredible, life-changing moment. I thought, *How is this possible? Am I going crazy?*

For some—or most—of you, this may have happened already. If so, you may know what I mean. However, for those who have not experienced it, you will. I promise that He will speak to your heart if you open it for Him. I strongly believe God will speak to your heart through this book.

God's
message
to
me

2

What did God say? God's first message to me was that He wanted me to teach a Bible study. I thought, *Why me, God? I know nothing about the Bible. As a matter of fact, I literally just finished reading my first book.*

God did not respond to my questions.

I got up from my chair and walked around the room, not understanding what was happening. It all felt unreal.

Another strong emotional feeling instructed me to obey God, and I felt the Holy Spirit's power to just trust in Him: "In you, Lord my God, in You I put my trust" (Psalm 25:1).

Within moments, I realized a miracle had happened. Feeling somewhat numb and in awe, I responded, "Okay, God, I'll do it, but You're going to have to help me because I have no idea what to do!"

I wanted to obey what God had just asked me to do. I grabbed a notebook and started planning. Teaching a Bible study was God's plan, and He was going to help me execute that plan. It was not my thought or plan; it was God's plan. I felt no fears, worries, or concerns. I allowed myself to put my whole trust in Him. Looking back, it was the most powerful and peaceful feeling I'd ever had. *Why haven't I fully trusted Him before—or ever?*

It was exactly God's plan. His plan was to lead me in how to do it. For the past seven years, God's thoughts and messages have become stronger and more frequent. As a matter of fact, to date, I have received 529 messages from God. I am sure He has sent messages to me for many years, but I never heard Him because I had not opened my heart for Him. I believed in Him, but I did not have a relationship with Him. Today, I put God first in my life. I want to fulfill my 2020 New Year's resolution of glorifying Him every chance I have.

At the end of this book is a topical index. This is a collection of Bible scriptures I have written on notecards and wear a scripture around my neck. "Let love and faithfulness never leave you; bind them around your neck and write them on the tablet of your heart." (Proverbs 3:3). I hope these Bible verses will help you in different situations. For example, when I need to remind myself about the feeling of peace that only comes from God, I review the Bible scriptures under "Trusting God."

My First Challenge

I am your Creator, you were in my care,
even before you were born.
—Isaiah 44:2 CEV

When God planned for me to start a Bible study, He knew that someone like me with a type A personality would face the challenge with wide-open arms. My "plans" always start with questions, and I came up with seven questions:

1. Where will I teach?
2. What time will I teach?
3. How do I start a Bible study?
4. Who am I going to teach?
5. What will I teach—and how will I teach it?
6. Will they even listen to me?
7. Why me, God?

To start the process, I reached out to two coworkers and asked if they would be interested in joining me for a women's Bible study. Surprisingly, they both said yes. During the next few days, I courageously walked around the office and asked a few more women, and they all said yes.

Oh no, I thought. *Am I really going to do this?*

The Holy Spirit guided me about who to ask, and 98 percent said yes. Some of you who are reading this book might remember that day.

Do I just ask the women—or should I include the men too?

I also asked the men, and God answered the first two questions:

- Where will I teach?
- What time will I teach?

I started researching workplace guidelines about discussing religion at work to make sure I abided by them. I discovered I needed to select a private room that was outside the workplace environment—and I found a solution. I decided to teach my Bible study in a small women's locker room that was adjacent to the women's restroom and outside the main office. I scheduled the Bible study during lunch hour. I thought, *No one can tell us what to do in a women's locker room during our lunch hour!*

The women sat on the shower bench and I stood. As the number of women surprisingly increased, some women used towels and sat on the concrete floor. At one moment I was standing, preaching, holding my materials, and kiddingly said "I need a podium." Well, one of the women surprised me showed up with my podium that she built. It was the most beautiful gift I have ever received!

Praying with my coworkers at work was a very touching and fulfilling experience for me. God has used me as a vessel to touch them through prayer. As the months went by, the number of attendees increased, launched an online Bible study, started sharing daily to weekly scriptures and even created a website.

I also started a monthly Bible study at home with a group of women. Throughout the years we have used this time to worship with each other, pray for one another and deepen our relationship with God through one another. God answered the second set of questions.

What and how to teach? Will they even listen to me?

I didn't really have a syllabus to follow and to be honest, I cannot recall what I taught the first time. It took me three years to finish reading and studying the entire Bible and my study notes became the syllabus. As time went on, God continued to place topics in my heart to teach and I just followed Him. It is a wonderful feeling when everyone who studies with me listens when I teach. God answered the third question.

- Why me, God?

God's plan was for me to be His vessel—to share and teach His Word through me. God knew I had always loved to teach, and He always had a plan for me to teach. About eleven years ago—after I received my MBA—I completed my teaching certification. At that time, I didn't even know why I enrolled for the certification, but looking back now, God wanted me to complete the teaching certification because teaching was His plan for me. God is amazing!

Seven Times Seven

God's first message to me to teach a Bible study was powerful. He continued to send me messages, and I wrote them on my journal. However, there was one message that He sent me on seven separate occasions, and I resisted His message each time. *What is wrong with me? How didn't I listen the first time?*

God's second most powerful message to me was to write this book. You would think I would have learned my lesson from the first message, but I questioned Him. *Why me, God? I'm not a very good writer.* I came up with multiple reasons not to write, but the most important reason was writing was my weakness. I hated writing papers while I was in college, but God was very persistent and just like His first message to me, I knew in my heart I needed to obey Him.

On July 2019, I celebrated the start of my seventh year of being saved. I announced that I was writing a book. The Bible taught me that I would overcome my weakness of not being a good writer through His grace:

But He has said to me, "My grace is sufficient for you: for power is being perfected in weakness." (2 Corinthians 12:9 AMP)

Miraculously, I now love writing! God is truly amazing! He gives me the strength and wisdom to write. I discipline myself and write at least an hour per day, and when I do, I feel so much more peaceful. It is hard to explain the feeling of joy in knowing I am obeying and glorifying God. It took a while to finish writing my book, but I finished it for God.

The Bible teaches us that the number seven is the most significant number because it is God's number. I thought it would be appropriate to plan for seven chapters, and I proposed a title for each chapter. When I look back at my life during the past seven years, my life experiences have been perfectly aligned with the title of each chapter. Was this a coincidence? Absolutely not. For my entire life, I have been living the plan God had for me—just like the movie *The Good, The Bad, and The Ugly.*

The Good

When I was seven years old, my parents courageously decided to migrate to the United States to provide my siblings and me the opportunity to live the American dream. My parents, my younger brother and sister, and I moved to Seattle. We were the first generation in the United States and the first to leave our family. Prior to our move, my father had been a vice president for a successful company in Manila. It was pretty impressive since he put himself through school by shining shoes in front of an office building. After many years, he climbed up the corporate ladder and became vice president of the exact same office building.

Moving into our first neighborhood in Seattle was a bit of a culture shock. At the time, there were only five minorities attending my school. I still remember the feeling of fear as I walked down the hall on my first day of school. My physical attributes were different from the other kids—my skin and hair color were darker, my eyes were more slanted, and I was shorter than everyone else—and I was alone. It felt like all the kids were staring at this little Asian girl. Most of my classmates lived in big, beautiful homes, and my family lived in a very small one-bedroom apartment on Seattle's famous Dravus Hill. My parents could not afford to purchase a house back then. We were starting a life in America as poor immigrants.

For seven years, my father worked three different jobs to provide enough income for our family. As experienced as my dad was, he still took a job as an entry-level accountant during the day, worked as a busboy at night, and worked overtime on the weekends. My mother had graduated with a teaching degree, but she stayed at home with my siblings and me.

When I was fourteen, I was given the responsibility of watching over my siblings after school so my mother could work a part-time job. When my parents saved enough money, we moved down south—where most Asians lived—and purchased our first home on Beacon Hill. Our house was small and old, but it was a place we called home for almost fifty years. Watching both of my parents working so hard was such an inspiration for me. I truly honored my father and my mother. I am a good and obedient daughter.

There were six families on my mother's side, and I had twenty-nine first cousins. We were taught by our grandparents that the eldest in each family had the responsibility of protecting and caring for the younger siblings. This tradition was passed down with each generation. As the eldest in our family, I learned this was my responsibility at an early age—and it has not changed to this day. I still watch over them and provide with the same unconditional love my parents have instilled in me. I am a good and protective big sister.

School was very easy for me. I had excellent grades and graduated with honors in high school, college, and graduate school.

On my first day of grade school, my mother said, "Show them that you are smarter than any of them."

As a young and obedient child, I followed her advice all the way until I walked across the stage for my MBA graduation and handed her my honors diploma. I was a good and well-behaved student.

At the age of five, my father noticed that I was extremely fond of writing numbers in between the spaces of a columnar pad. He knew I would become an accountant just like him. With his advice, I selected accounting as my college major and as a suitable career path.

My father said, "Every company needs an accountant—whether large or small, public or private—regardless of industry. They are all numbers—just different meanings." My father was so proud each time I moved up the corporate ladder in accounting and finance, and he continuously reminded me to "always work hard" and "do good at your job." To this day, I still have the same work ethic. I am a good and successful career woman.

Marriage came at the age of twenty-five to someone who had the complete opposite of my upbringing. We met at a tire store where he worked as a salesman. When I paid my bill that morning, I was mesmerized by his green eyes. We exchanged phone numbers, and thirty-two years later, we are still married. I am still mesmerized by his green eyes. Just like all marriages, we have had good times and bad times. The difference in our cultures played a big part in our relationship and raising our children. I was "book smart," and he was "street smart." The marriage vows we made are very sacred to me. I am a good and devoted wife.

We have two beautiful children, and our son and daughter are now adults with great careers ahead of them. Our daughter recently got married. My husband and I made a commitment that if we both had full-time jobs, our children would attend private Christian schools in order to obtain the best education and build a solid foundation for life. Having a social life and self-care—health and fitness—were not priorities for me. I wanted to be able to provide whatever my children needed, and I ignored my own needs. I am a good and loving mother.

The "good" part of my life was what I thought it was supposed to be. It was what I envisioned it should be—or at least that was what I understood. My plan was to be a good daughter, sister, student, career woman, wife, and mother. It was almost perfect, but I felt like something was missing. I felt like I was just keeping myself busy and going through the motions.

Can you take a few moments to think back all the good times in your life? Smile!

The Bad

Bad is defined as "of poor quality or a low standard." Similarly, it is also defined as "not as to be hoped for or desired." My "bad" years started during my adult life and reminded me of the song "It's a Hard Knock Life" from *Annie*.

When my life transitioned to adulthood, and I became a wife and mother, life felt hard. The devotion as a wife, the sacrifices and sleepless nights a mother must endure, and the financial responsibility of the household were quite overwhelming. I was no longer an eaglet resting comfortably in her parents' nest, and I had to fly on my own. I felt like I had lost control of what I needed to accomplish. That was a very conflicting and unwelcome feeling for a type A person.

My husband and I both had full-time jobs, but we were not very fiscally responsible. Sadly, as a finance person in charge of multimillion-dollar budgets for companies, I failed to be conservative with my own budget. Looking back, we could have saved so much money if we had spent wisely. When we had extra money, we were very quick to spend it. I was bad with handling our finances, which drove us to filing for bankruptcy in the early 1990s. I was a bad daughter and an embarrassment and a disappointment for my father.

My children experienced peer pressure while attending private schools from elementary through high school. Some of their classmates were from well-to-do families, and the stay-at-home moms drove fancier cars than I did. It was not just my children who felt peer pressure; I felt it too. Most of the stay-at-home moms looked down on the working moms. I wasn't going to allow them to look down on me, and I focused on climbing the corporate ladder. I wanted to earn more money in order to provide for my children and win their love "materially." Spending quality time with them was going to the mall. Did that make me a bad mom?

During this time, I felt like I was simply going through the motions. I call them the "bad years" because I could not seem to overcome it—no matter how hard I tried. Adult responsibility was too much to bear. *Why am I not surviving? Why am I not smart enough to be fiscally responsible? Why is God punishing me if I was good before? Is He punishing me?*

The Bible teaches us that God doesn't punish anyone. He forgives us when we admit our sins, and He forgives us even before we sin. However, we must also admit our own weaknesses and wrongdoings, which can be difficult. I always thought people would look down or think of me as a failure if I admitted my faults. This was especially true in my relationship with my husband. I always had to be correct with him, and even if I were wrong, I would never admit I was wrong, which led to many arguments. The words "I'm sorry" were not part of my vocabulary. Today, I am more at ease to saying, "I'm sorry" or "My apologies." I ask God for forgiveness, especially when I feel He has convicted me or reminded me of any wrongdoings.

Is it hard or easy for you to apologize when you have done something wrong?

Anthony: Let God be the Center of your Life

> We are afflicted in every way, but not crushed;
> perplexed, but not driven to despair; persecuted, but
> not forsaken; struck down but not destroyed.
> —2 Corinthians 4:8–9 (ESV)

Anthony, a fun, loving, and strong man in his fifties, recently celebrated his silver (twenty-fifth) wedding anniversary. He has two adult children. Anthony was raised as a "holiday Catholic," and his family only attended Mass during the holidays. During his teenage years, his father decided to be with a younger woman, leaving behind Anthony's mother as a single woman raising four children. I had the opportunity to meet Anthony's mom, and the similarities are remarkable. His mother is a fun, loving, and courageous woman. Her brave heart is as big as Anthony's when it comes to family.

The divorce of Anthony's parents devastated him and had an impact during his teenage years. He felt betrayed that his father had left them, and he was not too fond that his father's new wife. She had a son who was able to live with his father. Because of that, Anthony's resentment of his father, new stepmother, and new stepbrother grew. I felt the sadness in his heart as he was telling me his story. We were sitting in a loud, crowded restaurant during my interview, but I could hear the sadness in the cracks in his voice. His mom's pain broke his heart, and losing the man he was supposed to look up to made it even worse.

Anthony loved playing sports during his school years. Unfortunately, his father showed little interest and rarely attended his games. The multiple disappointments Anthony had to accept became the norm, but mother was always there for him. When he reached high school, he felt pressure from his friends to smoke cigarettes, and he discovered alcohol as an escape for his problems at home. How sad to be that young, feeling disappointed and alone.

Anthony was ready for a new journey—a journey with no more disappointments.

After high school, he joined the military. He thought his father might be proud of how brave and mature Anthony had become. Anthony learned a lot about discipline, and he thrived in the military. For his graduation, his father promised to attend and celebrate with Anthony and his friends, but his father did not show up. When he shared this with me, it reminded me of a scene from *An Officer and a Gentleman.* Right after graduation, while everyone was celebrating and hugging their families, Richard Gere was alone, looking around for someone or something. I had a vision of Anthony doing the same thing. Was he looking for his father who promised to be there? Another big disappointment.

After the military, he moved to a different state and met his future wife, Marie. Anthony maintained a distant relationship with his father, and when he got married, he asked his father to be the best man. However, his father did not approve of his wife because she was not American. His father claimed Anthony "could have done better." During the wedding reception, his father went to a nearby bar instead of joining the celebration. Another disappointment. The disappointments never seemed to dissipate.

However, Anthony never gave up. He continued to try to get closer to his father, but he showed little or no interest. Marie said, "It was like watching a grown-up man with a heart of a little boy still waiting for his father to return or wanting his father to be like other fathers. A reality that he knew would take a miracle to happen."

Anthony and Marie's early years of marriage were unsteady, and God was not the center of their new life. Anthony held a blue-collar job and enjoyed his time drinking and spending time at bars with his coworkers. When he got injured at his job, the doctor prescribed pain medications. Anthony mixed them with his drinks, and he eventually became addicted. "I used anything that would alter my mind," Anthony said. He became focused on having a good time, and he enjoyed wild activities and drinking feasts with his friends.

It was another way of altering his mind. I wonder if Anthony felt guilty and thought that the many disappointments of his dad were his fault for not being a good son.

While he was in his late forties, things got worse for Anthony emotionally. "I became depressed and cheated on my wife. I even had suicidal thoughts," Anthony admitted. His infidelity almost ended his marriage, but his wife gave him another chance. His children looked at him differently after the truth came out, but those feelings started to improve after the family went to counseling. They all wanted to be a happy family.

As he turned fifty, the idea of a midlife crisis bothered him, but instead, it became a midlife rebirth. He found God and proclaimed him as his Savior, and God became the center of his life. Today, he spends time every morning listening to God's Word while he gets ready for work. His marriage is healthy, and his love for his wife is stronger than ever. They attend service every week, enjoy their life together, and are looking forward to retirement. For the first time in Anthony's life, after the many disappointments caused by his father and his own mistakes of infidelity and immaturity, he believes God has finally given him a new journey.

Life can be full of disappointments. Disappointments can mean darkness to some people. Anthony chose not to stay in the dark, and he followed his heart. This is such an inspiring story about someone who never gave up on love:

> But I say to you, do not resist an evil person. If anyone slaps you on your right cheek, turn the other cheek also. (Matthew 5:39 NIV)

God never leaves us or forsakes us. I believe God was the center of Anthony's life all along, but he just didn't know it. He had been practicing what God had placed in his loving heart to do all those years.

Have you experienced similar disappointment in your own

family? Can we be patient and loving like Anthony? Do not stay in the dark—and remember that God is the center of our lives!

Stella: A Moment in Time

> Be wise in the way you act toward outsiders;
> make the most of every opportunity.
> —Colossians 4:5 (NIV)

The first time I met Stella was when I approached her at the grocery store.

"Are you the lady who works in our accounting department?" I asked.

She responded, "Yes."

I asked how she commuted to work, and Stella let me know that she drove alone every day. We worked about thirty miles away from our neighborhood, and the thirty-mile commute can take an hour or more, especially during rush hour.

At the time, I managed a van pool as a way of commuting to work, and I asked her to join us, which would save her time, wear and tear on her car, and gas money.

Stella graciously accepted and became a member of our van pool. That one moment of kindness led to a warm and tender relationship that Stella and I still enjoy.

I got to know Stella through our van pool, and we sometimes drove alone together, which built our relationship. She has been married to her loving husband, Carlo, for more than thirty years. She has two adult children and two adorable grandchildren. Stella continued to work full-time for a few more years and then "officially retired," which means she continued to work a few hours a week. I often tease her about that and believe she will never fully retire. When I officially retire, I will probably follow in Stella's footsteps and work a few hours a week—but not in the office. I will most likely work part-time at a shopping mall so I can surround myself with happy people. I think people are much happier when they are at shopping malls, and I often find myself needing "retail therapy."

I never thought Stella had experienced any bad times, but she had. One morning, we met at a coffee shop, and she told me that her bad years started when her marriage to her first husband did not work. Before that day, we had never really discussed that part of her life. Her second marriage to Carlo is much better, and they are still happily married. People who see the love they have for each other can only wish they could feel the same love. They are both retired, and they both enjoy traveling. When they are not traveling, Stella works part-time. Carlo has a morning ritual of rowing on Lake Washington with his buddies. He is probably the most physically fit man I know who is in his sixties.

Stella's situation might not seem bad, but her current challenge is a common one. Stella is Christian, and she worships and loves God. Her son is also a believer. He worships God by sharing his talent of playing drums, and he is in charge of organizing all the events and videos for his congregation. Carlo is also a believer—but not of God. Instead, he believes in science. His beliefs are based on facts, and he needs clear evidence before he can believe. When they got married, they did not really discuss their beliefs, and they were not a priority during that time. Stella did not think it would cause a challenge in their marriage if they had such a strong love for each other.

Today, Stella is hurting inside. She cannot understand why her husband will not go to church. "How can anyone not put God first in their life?" Stella asked. Stella regrets that she never discussed God or church prior to her second marriage. As a faithful believer, Stella continues to attend services without Carlo. It is something she has accepted, and she knows it will not change. People don't change; only God can change Carlo's heart.

Do you have loved ones who you are trying to persuade to believe in God or attend a service with you? Do you feel sad and find yourself wondering what or how they deal with bad situations?

It is heartbreaking to know that someone you love and care about does not know the Lord. Who do they seek and what do they do to help them get through hard times? The best and only way I know is to pray for them faithfully and consistently. Let me share a prayer I wrote:

Prayer for a Nonbeliever

Almighty Father in heaven
I solemnly pray to You today.
And it breaks my heart to say
There is someone in my life
Who does not believe in You.

Your love is precious
An unconditional love for us.
How can anyone turn away
And not believe?

Father God, please hear my prayer.
I pray for (insert name of person) today
That You touch his/her heart
Just like You touched mine.

May he/she listen to Your voice
And believe in the Holy Spirit's guidance.
For Your love for us is here, and it is real.
And it will always be, for all eternity.
I believe in Jesus's name. Amen.

Elizabeth: When Will the Loneliness Vanish?

> But let him ask in faith, with no doubting, for the one who doubts
> is like a wave of the sea that is driven and tossed by the wind.
> —James 1:6 (ESV)

Elizabeth and I met through a mutual friend, Margaret. Elizabeth is a lovely lady and has two lovely children. When we were first introduced, she instantly made me feel as if we had been friends for a long time. Along with her vibrant personality, Elizabeth is a foreigner who speaks with an accent that draws you to her and makes you just want to listen to her talk. She can communicate openly about whatever is on her mind.

It has been many years since Elizabeth experienced a painful divorce, but she is still challenged by her loneliness. When her ex-husband remarried, her loneliness worsened. Her memories of the divorce made it feel like someone had stabbed her heart twice.

"Why did he deserve to find someone—and I did not?" Elizabeth asked.

Her divorce reminds me of another close friend whose parents divorced while he was young. He has witnessed the bitterness of his mother toward his father for the past forty years. How can someone be that bitter and unforgiving for such a long time? Was the feeling that painful?

At least thirty-three scriptures in the Bible teach us about the sacredness of marriage, but American divorce rates are still high. As a matter of fact, a recent publication from the American Psychological Association showed the divorce rate of married couples in the United States is as high as 40 to 50 percent. There are many justifiable reasons for a marriage to break, but it is disturbing to see a rate that high.

I almost filed for a divorce ten years ago, but I was reminded of the wedding vow I made to God. My husband committed adultery. It was extremely difficult to forgive him, but God is merciful and gave me the strength to not follow through with the divorce. He continues to give me strength when the painful memory haunts me. I am very familiar with the pain Elizabeth is challenged with, and I have doubted myself the same way she does many times.

Today, Elizabeth continues to pray for a man to share the rest of her life with. A friend of hers is in the same situation and is also looking for a companion. The difference between the two friends is their belief in God. Her friend is a Spiritualist and not Christian. She prays a lot—but not to Jesus—and eventually found a man to be with.

Elizabeth said, "It frustrates me that she doesn't pray and is able to meet someone. Why me, God?" She is frustrated and does not understand why He is not answering her prayers. She is tired of feeling bad.

When we pray, we sometimes want instant gratification. However, sometimes, another event will occur to compound the pain. That is enemy trying to distract us from praying. He wants us to lose our patience and start doubting God, but we must not do that. God will rescue us and hear our prayers—no matter what they are. In His perfect timing, as He has repeatedly showed me, He will answer our prayers. He will help us find someone, provide funds to help us with financial difficulties, heal our broken hearts, or mend our relationships with family or friends. We must fight the good fight of faith.

When we go through trials, we must fight the enemy constantly by praying faithfully and reading the Bible to remind ourselves of God's promises and writing. I quiet myself and listen to God's healing voice because God is my Savior. I have learned many lessons about not doubting God. I focus and patiently wait for Him to deliver me in His own amazingly perfect timing. I practice what I preach and believe wholeheartedly. God will undoubtedly provide the peace and joy for my friend Elizabeth—and for all of us.

Are you experiencing doubts about yourself and/or God? What do you think you can do other than praying to help you fight the good fight of faith? Is He asking you to take care of others while He takes care of us?

God Is Our Author

> You saw me before I was born. Every day of my
> life was recorded in your book. Every moment
> was laid out before a single day had passed.
> —Psalm 139:16 (NLT)

With God's leading, I became a writer and was blessed with another opportunity to be a vessel for Him. I consider this message an opportunity and not an obligation. I already know that writing is not going to be a simple task, but I have to "fight the good fight of faith" (1 Timothy 6:12 AMP). I know God will provide me the wisdom and hold my hand until my book is finished.

We experience good times and bad times in our lives. The Bible teaches us that our lives may not be perfect, but we should always enjoy them and not just go through the motions. I have discovered that the enjoyment of our lives is directly correlated to our relationship with God.

God loves us unconditionally. He is beside us every second of the day. He never leaves us or forsakes us. Nothing is impossible when we believe, have faith, and put our hope in Him. What does it take to enjoy the life that God has promised us? God wants us to have a relationship with Him. What does it mean to have a relationship with God? How does it feel when you have—or don't have—a relationship with Jesus? How do we know?

Our relationship with God can be analyzed with a LIFE (Living In Faith Everyday) graph. The target line of the LIFE graph is our relationship with God. Dropping below the line means we do not have a relationship with Him, and rising above the line means we do.

My LIFE graph is shown below. I was amazed and in awe when I discovered the correlation of my life experiences and my relationship with God. Building a relationship with God and reaching spiritual maturity takes time, and that is okay. God is patient with us. He was very patient with me—and He still is. There are still times when I forget Him or forget to do what He has asked me to do. I still make my mistakes—the same mistakes He has convicted me of before—but He has also forgiven me because I matter to Him. There are no more bad times. There are just good times. It is all good. Please take the time to review the LIFE graph below. (A blank graph is available in appendix A to create your own).

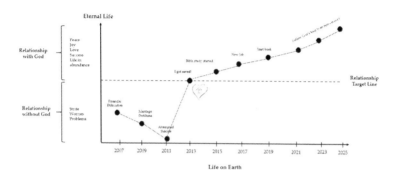

Do I even matter? Yes, you do!

> It is because of the Lord's mercy and loving kindness that we are not consumed because His compassion never fails. They are new every morning; great and abundant is Your stability and faithfulness. The Lord is my portion and my inheritance therefore I have hope in Him and wait expectantly for Him. (Lamentations 3:22–26 AMP)

We all matter to God, and He has a plan for you—just as He did for Anthony, Stella, Elizabeth, and me. The enemy blinds us from His plan, especially during the bad times, but God is always there. He will continue to lead us. His compassion never fails. Rise every morning and be excited to see what God has in store for you that day!

Do I Even Matter?

Notes from Chapter 1

- Have your plans in the past worked?
- What are your plans and dreams for the future?

CHAPTER 2

Staying in the Dark

I create the light and make the darkness. I send good times and
bad times. I, the Lord, am the one who does these things.
—Isaiah 45:7 (NLT)

Have you ever heard people say, "There's a dark cloud hanging over
me"? Have you ever stayed in the dark, feeling afraid, hopeless, and
alone?

What Does Dark Look Like?

As I shared in the previous chapter, I have had good years and bad
years. After going through the bad years, I thought it couldn't get
any worse—but it did. The ugly years started to creep up. During
the ugly times, I was unhealthy and carried a heavy wounded heart.
I lived through the darkest moments of my life.

The Ugly

We purchased a beautiful, brand-new home in 2005. It was a model
home in our subdivision, which included all the special furnishings,

installations, interior fixtures, and custom upgrades that buyers can select from when purchasing a home. Our home had all the bells and whistles. It had six bedrooms, three bathrooms, a formal dining room, a formal living room, and a family room. It had more space than we ever wanted. The interior design of our house and the furniture layout met our expectations. It had a very small yard, which was fine because neither my husband nor I enjoyed yard work. The house was located on a corner lot and was within walking distance of the park. Our children enjoyed playing with the other neighborhood kids. It was my dream home, and we could reasonably afford it. The only setback was that the front door faced west.

In the Asian culture, which my mother reminded me about when we purchased the house, it brings good luck if the main door of the house faces east because that is where the sun rises. It is believed that the brightness of the sun indicates a bright future and will bless the homeowners with wealth and progress in life. I considered it a silly superstition and ignored my cultural beliefs. However, my ugly years started after we purchased the house, and they stretched out for several years. I started to think differently about the superstition. It felt as if the suffering was confined to my beautiful "dark" home.

Just as the Israelites wandered in the wilderness for forty years to find their way to the Promised Land, I wandered in my wilderness for several years too. It felt like I was just going through the motions as a wife, mother, and career woman, day in and day out. I started every day worrying about everything, and when I went to bed, I worried about the next day. It was a never-ending cycle. My life was a daily task list, and I checked off the tasks when I completed them. The sad part was that I did not feel satisfied when I had completed the tasks. Instead, I remained frustrated and sad.

Relationship

On May 6 1989, I married my first love. My wedding vows were sacred: "In sickness and in health, until death do us part." We met at the tire store where he worked, and I was completely mesmerized by his green eyes when we exchanged phone numbers. We dated for a year, and he said, "You are fun to be with."

My husband started living on his own when he turned eighteen, and he thrived on living independently. On the contrary, I was very dependent on my parents and lived with them until I got married. My husband and I had a lot of adjusting to do during the early years of our marriage due to the differences in our upbringings. We were challenged by how to communicate effectively. We had moments where our ways of communication involved calling each other descriptive names, yelling, and blaming each other. I was no longer "fun to be with." *Why is marriage so hard? My parents had a wonderful marriage. Why is mine suffering? Life is dark.*

The strife and unhappiness at home led my husband in a different direction, and he sought a more peaceful relationship. A married woman at work who I identified as "the vulture" decided to chase him around because her husband was "no fun either." It seemed that they were both unhappy with their spouses, and their common need sparked a relationship, which ended up in an affair. When the truth came out, I was deeply hurt, devastated, and betrayed. I was weak, confused, and lost. I felt sorry for myself. My dark life started to turn darker.

That time of darkness lasted for many miserable years. My faith was intact, and I believed it would get better someday. I was committed to stay married because I had made a vow in front of God to stay with my husband "in sickness and in health, until death do us part." It was not easy, and I felt uncomfortable at times, but I also had to think about the welfare of our children. I didn't want my children to grow up in a divorced family, separated during holidays, and go through what my husband went through when his parents divorced. Staying in the dark means having a relationship with someone while keeping the disturbing feelings inside.

I asked God why He was punishing me when all I had done was be a good and devoted wife—or was I?

It was God's plan for me to live in the dark during that time. I didn't understand, and I was too blind to see what was happening. I was too blind to see my own faults or admit them. All I could see was that it was all my husband's fault—and that I was "perfect." During our arguments, even though he was right, I would not admit it. I preferred to argue even more. It takes two people to ruin a relationship, and I was focused on my husband's faults and how I could change him. *I'm perfect, and there is nothing wrong with me. My husband is the one who needs to change.* Sadly, I truly believed that my bad behavior was the solution that would make our marriage work. Staying in the dark means not admitting your faults or weaknesses.

While my marriage was falling apart, our teenage children were going through their peer pressure years. It was not a loving and comfortable home for them to live in. They had their own needs and school obligations to focus on. Most of their classmates had stay-at-home moms who could cater to their every need, but I was just the opposite. I was a working career-driven woman who didn't know how to spend quality time with my own children.

My daily routine was to get up in the morning, drop them off at school, and go to work. In the evening, we ate dinner and went to bed with absolutely no quality time. During the weekends, I did errands, and on Sundays, I pretty much forced my children to attend Mass. It was an ugly period of my life because I was too busy and unaware of the importance of spending quality time with the two most precious gifts God had given me. Staying in the dark means forgetting the treasures God provides.

Career

My father taught me to always maintain a good work ethic, and I followed his advice. However, since I am "perfect," when I reached the management level, I behaved very aggressively and was very controlling in the workplace for many years. I walked around with my nose up in the air because I was successfully climbing the corporate ladder.

While my father was proud of my accomplishments, the feedback from my team made me realize I was "the vulture." Sound familiar? "Do not judge, or you too will be judged" (Matthew 7:1 NIV). I talked condescendingly to many of my coworkers and was disrespectful of others. I was annoyed if a coworker did not perform their work as "perfectly" as I could. Staying in the dark means bragging and boasting about yourself and placing judgment on others.

The Darkest of all Times

The ugly, unhealthy, and difficult relationships with my family, career, and everything around me became darker during the darkest time. No one listened or heard me as I cried out for help. *Doesn't anyone appreciate everything I do?* I felt hopeless, emotionally drained, heartbroken, physically weak, and alone. I had lost control of my emotions and mind, and I had nothing left to give.

My life felt like a roller coaster on a rapid decline after a steep upward climb or a volcano that was about to erupt. In the middle of the night, I got into my car, drove to grocery store's parking lot, and screamed and cried. In my distress, I finally called upon the Lord: "Why, God? Why?" I had hit rock bottom, and the only solution I could see was to end my life. Staying in the dark means there was no reason for me to live—and no more love to give or feeling love in return. *No one cares about me. Do I even matter?*

The Truth about Suicide

Suicide is not a comfortable topic, and it is not easily discussed. The ugly period of my life was the toughest and darkest, and it pushed me over the edge. Suicidal thoughts started, and I welcomed the concept. The mind-set of a person who reaches that point is numb and unclear. My only focus was the fact that life was hopeless and there was no need to live any longer. The thought of attempting suicide became more favorable as the days went on. The only challenge was selecting the method.

The first of my three attempts was consuming a handful of sleeping pills. I did not want to get hurt; I just wanted to sleep to my painless death. *Why should I suffer? I sacrificed my life for all of them.* My husband found me in bed with the open bottle of sleeping pills by my side, and he called the medics. Instead of dying, I got a slap on the wrist and went back to staying in the dark.

The second suicide attempt was consuming a handful of pain medication (muscle relaxers) to make the suicide more effective and successful. It was supposed to be less painful because I would feel relaxed. My husband found me again and called the medics, and I ended up in the emergency room. That time, I was scolded by my family, which did not go over very well with me because they were the reason I was in the ER. *My family was not there to help me—or were they?*

You might think that two suicide attempts would get my family's attention, but they all thought I was mentally ill. I was back in the dark again, which led me to my final and most serious attempt.

The third suicide attempt was carefully planned out. I just had the urge to disappear. I drove to my parents' house since "no one at my own house cared about me." People who are about to commit suicide need to say their goodbyes, and I left voice mails for my family. I received an immediate reaction after my voice mails, which meant they were listening. It felt good. *My plan is working.*

My parents were not home when I arrived, which was perfect

because I wanted them to find me dead anyway. I went to my old bedroom with a gigantic knife, but I was scared. I really did not want to feel any pain or see any blood, but it was my third attempt—and it could not fail. I tried to slit a wrist, but I did not do it hard enough. I had to try again. *Oh no, the next one is really going to hurt.* And it did. I passed out. Success! Staying the dark means feeling hopeless and alone, and the only solution is to end life.

Obviously, my plan failed. I woke up in a padded room in a hospital psychiatric unit and was completely disappointed that I was alive. I don't know who found me—the topic was never discussed after the incident—but the police officers broke down my parents' door to get into the house and called the ambulance. Somehow my family figured out where I was. Evidently, my disappearing act had failed.

When my family visited me in the hospital, I saw the looks of disappointment and sadness in their eyes as they tried to understand what had happened and how I had been in such despair. When my husband and brother-in-law visited, I had no words and felt emotionless. My parents looked helpless and extremely sad. My brother and son couldn't visit; it was way too painful and beyond comprehension for them.

My daughter's and sister's visits were the hardest and resonated with me the most. My daughter said, "I need my mother at my wedding."

My sister mentioned my nieces and said, "Who will look after Jamie and Vangie?"

The entire experience crushed me. *Am I back in the dark again?*

Eddie: Peaks and Valleys

Even though I walk through the valley of death, I shall fear no evil. For You are with me, Your rod and staff they comfort me.
—Psalm 23:4 (ESV)

Eddie and I were introduced a couple of years ago, and I am honored to have become a mentor for him. He lives on the East Coast, and I live on the West Coast. We are on opposite sides of the United States, but we share the same love for Jesus. There was a moment that really bonded the two of us, and it was after one of our phone conversations when he wanted to close our call by asking if we could say a prayer together. That was the first time someone had asked me to pray after a work meeting, and it was a special moment.

Eddie was not born a Christian, and he describes his life in two stages. The first was his life before he became Christian, and he transitioned to the second stage when he followed God. I had always wondered what nonbelievers do when they don't have God in their lives, and Eddie shared that with me. Growing up as a nonbeliever and at school as a teenager, he was solely focused on winning. His parents wanted him to get straight A's, and anything else would make him feel less valuable. To hope to win was not just a practice; instead, it was a strict mind-set to win. Hope does not resonate with nonbelievers. Without hope, there's no disappointment. I am the only one to blame. I am too busy to think about hope. That is something I need to worry about later.

Eddie looked back at how he started to follow Jesus and said, "Reflection is a gift from God." Prior to Eddie's move to the East Coast to attend grad school as an international student, his best friend, Bob, suggested and introduced him to a Bible study group. Bob thought it would be a good way for Eddie to meet other people since he would be alone without his family.

Bob had always wanted Eddie to be open-minded about Christianity. For someone who was alone in a strange country, faced with a culture shock, Eddie was a courageous young man. He was about to begin a hard curriculum, and he decided to join a Bible study group with other young believers in the school cafeteria. Eddie's courage stems from his old mind-set of winning, being the best, and making his parents proud of him. If you recall, Eddie's upbringing and mind-set were identical to my upbringing. Eddie thrived in grad school, received excellent grades, met new friends, and received a job offer right out of school. His parents were so proud of him. Eddie had reached his "peak of happiness."

At Eddie's highest peak, he received two notifications that made him feel like he was starting to fall off the peak at a very rapid pace. While Eddie was not familiar with the phrase "a dark cloud hanging over me," his life seemed dark. He received two notices within the same week, and if not met, Eddie would have to leave the United States. Additional supporting documentation was required to validate his continuance to stay, and at the same time, his student visa was due to expire within thirty days.

Time was immediately shortened, and Eddie was on critical path to depart. It was unacceptable and incomprehensible for him, but the disappointment became a reality. Worst of all, Eddie's parents flew in to watch him graduate—only to find out he had to return home soon without hope of ever returning to the United States. Eddie called his friends, lawyers, and brothers and sisters for advice, but no one was able to provide comfort. Eddie had sleepless nights, and everything seemed to be out of control. Eddie was thinking about the paths God had planned for him.

Eddie went back to China the day before his visa expired. Eddie's first month at home was not as productive as he had hoped it would be. His time spent studying the Bible was at a minimum, and he kept himself distant from others. However, he did not stay in the dark. During his second month at home, Eddie bounced back, started to look for a job in a major city, and searched for a Christian church to attend. He quickly found a church and a job. Later, Eddie was presented with an opportunity to come back to the United States and continue working. Eddie was beyond ecstatic to return to the United States.

Today, Eddie maintains that big smile on his face and is thriving at a large organization, surrounded by his new loving wife and friends. He continues to practice Christianity, and his love for Jesus has grown stronger. Eddie wants to share two lessons from his story:

"It is one thing to practice, but to experience God during a difficult time is more of a blessing than a test. God prepares us with all the options."

Let us all be reminded that a disappointment—or darkness—can happen when we are at our highest peaks of happiness, but God is always there. He will never leave us or forsake us. God will never let us stay in the dark. In fact, the darkness will let God's grace shine even brighter. Press on, dear brothers and sisters. Press on with the strength from our heavenly Father.

Samantha: A Cry for Help

> In my distress I called upon the Lord; to my God,
> I cried for help. From His temple, he heard my
> voice and my cry to Him reached his ears.
> —Psalm 18:6 (ESV)

Samantha is a beautiful and smart young lady. I had an opportunity to visit with her today, and coincidentally, it was during the time I was writing this chapter. It is amazing how God brings people together.

Samantha is currently living in the dark. She ended a relationship with a serious long-distance boyfriend, her job situation is not working well—she works for a controlling manager who is not interested in developing his team—her uncle who she is close with was recently diagnosed with Stage 4 cancer, and she has no family in the state she currently lives in. Samantha feels the darkness over her, and at most times, it feels overwhelming. She stays awake all night and has a hard time getting herself to go to work. When she makes it to work, she finds herself tired, depressed, and wanting to cry.

The great thing about my conversation with Samantha was her faith. As I listened to her, I hated the enemy more and more: "That enemy of yours, the devil, prowls around like a roaring lion seeking someone to devour" (1 Peter 5:8 AMP). In Samantha's case, the enemy devours and weakens her.

Samantha and I combined our thoughts about how to continually fight the enemy. Let us all "fight the good fight of faith" (1 Timothy 6:12 NIV). We came up with five things to focus on:

1. Stop feeling sorry for yourself
2. "God, what are you trying to teach me in this situation?"
3. Join a Bible study group
4. Participate in fellowship at church
5. Constantly remind yourself that your time earth is meant to be learning and doing God's work in preparation for eternal life

Would you be willing to try one or more of these ways to fight the enemy with us?

Listening to Samantha brought back the situations I was in when I stayed in the dark. It is so easy to believe the enemy during the dark times, and it is so hard to worship when you are suffering. Believe me, I know. Samantha is tired of crying, and she is determined to fight the enemy. Months have passed since our discussion, and Samantha is no longer crying. God heard her cries and wiped away her tears. She knows how to fight the enemy:

> Finally, be strong in the Lord and in his mighty power. Put on the full armor of God, so that you can take your stand against the devil's schemes. (Ephesians 6:10–11 NIV)

Can you use God's shoulder to cry on? Lean on Him—and cry your heart out to Him. He will wipe away your tears.

Andrew: Not Meant to be Broken

The Lord is near to the brokenhearted. And
saves those who are crushed in spirit.
—Psalm 34:18 (NIV)

Andrew is a young man who grew up in an Asian culture like I did. Asians are taught at a very young age to never break the strong bond of our families and respect for our elders. At a young age, Andrew started working in the family business. It taught him discipline and perseverance. His family lived in a custom-made dream home because of their hard earnings and lived comfortably. It was "perfect."

Time passed, and his parents started to experience relationship issues. These issues became worse and eventually reached the point of emotional and financial breakdowns. His parents filed for bankruptcy, sold all their assets, lost their dream home, and were on the verge of a divorce, which is not a common practice in our culture. A divorce is almost considered a taboo and will break the one thing that can never be broken: the family bond. Andrew was devastated, and it was a time in his life when the darkest of the clouds were above him. Thankfully, his parents' relationship improved, and they did not divorce. Andrew's family is still intact, and his family's bond did not break.

Andrew experienced other circumstances where he felt that there was a dark cloud hanging over him. When his family's bond was about to break, his faith in God was strong. He knew that whatever was happening was not permanent. In his heart, Andrew knew God had a plan for him. Andrew does not stay in the dark; he keeps a strong faith, practices not comparing himself to others, and has learned a lot from his experiences. Andrew said, "I have had the feeling of darkness in my life—and I still do—but I know everything is temporary and has its purpose in molding me into the person I am supposed to be."

Do you believe our trials are temporary? Would you be able to keep a strong faith while going through trials?

God Is Our Comforter

> Praise be to the God and Father of our Lord Jesus Christ, the Father of compassion and the God of all comfort, who comforts us in all our troubles.
> —2 Corinthians 1:3–5 (NIV)

Life on earth is temporary—and thank goodness it is only temporary. During our time on earth, we will experience trials, hardships, sufferings, and the death of loved ones. We will feel like there is a dark cloud hanging over us and following us. I think of the dark cloud as the enemy hovering over the soul, body, and mind to the point of suffocation. We are in a state of mourning or deep sorrow.

We are feeling sorry for ourselves because nothing seems to be working and/or nobody cares. All these feelings are temporary because God cares:

> Blessed are those who mourn for they shall be comforted (Matthew 5:4 NIV)

This is another reminder of how God comforts us. Our inability to maintain strong faith during the hard times is the power of the enemy. The enemy wants us to stay in the dark and not see the light. We must not stay in the dark; we need to see past it to where God is. He is your light, and He will fight your battle.

> You will not have to fight this battle. Take up your positions; stand firm and see the deliverance the Lord will give you … Do not be afraid; do not be

discouraged. Go out to face them tomorrow, and the Lord will be with you. (2 Chronicles 20:17)

Do I even matter? Yes, you do!

> But as for me, I will look expectantly to the Lord and with confidence in Him, I will keep watch; I will wait for the God of my salvation; my God will hear me. Do not rejoice over me, O my enemy! When I fall, I will rise; Though I sit in darkness, the Lord is a light for me.
> —Micah 7:7–8 (AMP)

We all matter to God, and He wants Eddie, Samantha, Andrew, and you—and me—to stay out of the dark. God wants us to enjoy our lives while we are here on earth. There is so much peace and happiness that only comes from Him—and much, much more when we join Him in heaven. May you rise and walk toward the light to meet God. He is there, and He will always be there waiting for you!

Do I Even Matter?

Notes from Chapter 2

- Have you ever heard people say, "There's a dark cloud hanging over me"?
- Have you ever stayed in the dark, feeling afraid, hopeless, and alone?

CHAPTER 3

Let There Be Light

Again, Jesus spoke to them, saying, "I am the light
of the world. Whoever follows me will not walk
in darkness but will have the light of life."
—John 8:12 (ESV)

What is the symbol of light for you? Does it mean hope? Does it
mean peace? Does it mean it is God?

Finding the Light

When my daughter was a toddler, each time she coughed, my
husband and I would always say "Look up, look up, look up at the
light." Why is that? Why the light? Is it because looking up at the
light brings hope to end the cough?

Light illuminates darkness. If you walk through your backyard
or the woods at night, you will need a flashlight to see the way. Some
of us may have night-lights in our houses to guide us if we get up
in the middle of the night. When we arrive late to a movie theater,
guiding lights on the floor will help us find our seats. That's what a
light does. It illuminates the darkness to help us find our way.

God's Word also illuminates the darkness in our lives. His Word gives us hope and will lead us to the path He wants to shine on us. God wants to show us the Way, the Truth, and the Life through His Word. When we obey His Word, we are following God. When we are following God, we will find the light of life that only comes from Him. He is the light of the world. God is the light.

Turning On the Light

It was a quiet morning, and I was quietly strapped to my hospital bed in the psychiatric unit. I could see a crack of light from the hallway under the door, and with great disappointment, I realized where I was. *What happened to me? How did I end up here? Why has God punished me? Where do I go from here?*

Moments later, the nurse slowly opened my door and turned on the light. "It is time to get ready for the day, Sofia. You need to attend a class after breakfast."

"A class? What class?" I asked.

"It's a life-changing class, and it will help you."

As you can imagine, I was not thrilled to hear that I had to attend a class with a bunch of psych patients. I frowned and mumbled, "I don't belong with them."

I am already depressed about being here, and I do not want to talk to anyone. I just want to crawl back in bed after breakfast and be even more depressed and feel sorry for myself that I failed at the third attempt to end my life. I tried making excuses to skip the class, but I was afraid of disobeying the nurse. She reminded me of Nurse Ratched from *One Flew over the Cuckoo's Nest.*

Moving extremely slowly, I finished eating breakfast and returned to my room. There wasn't really any getting ready for the day because I was not allowed to wear any makeup or change out of my oversized, unattractive hospital gown.

Nurse Ratched came back to my room and said, "Please hurry, the class is about to start."

With heavy frustration and complete disgust, I slowly grabbed my thin hospital robe and opened the door to attend the class. As I made my way to the classroom, I noticed the brightness of the lights in the hallway. My eyes were very sensitive, and bright lights give me a headache. I became even more annoyed because I didn't have my sunglasses to minimize the glare. *This is not going to be a good day,* I thought.

Well, my thought was completely wrong. The life-changing class really did change me. I found myself completely engaged in the discussions, and I enjoyed conversing with my fellow patients. We came from all walks of life, but even with the unsteadiness of our emotional and mental well-being, we shared one thing in common. We were all longing for someone to pay attention to us. We were all longing for our loved ones to let us know we were loved.

We had to take several classes before we could "graduate" out of the psych unit and be discharged into the "general population." We all became friends and supported each other. During our hospital stays, we were able to give each other the attention we all longed for. Unfortunately, it was against hospital policy to exchange personal contact information, and we were not allowed to have connections with each other after discharge.

My hospital stay turned out to be the most pivotal point of my life! God showed me that He is the light. He was the light I saw under the door. He was the light that was turned on by Nurse Ratched, and He was the bright lights in the hallway. Was Nurse Ratched a disguise for God? He was shining His light on me. I found God within the compounds of a psych unit in a hospital. God has turned on my light of life. He has turned it on to show me the Way.

The Way

> Jesus answered, I am the Way, the Truth, and the Life.
> No one comes to the Father except through Me.
> —John 14:6 (NIV)

On the day of my discharge from the hospital, I had mixed feelings. I felt "healed," but I was not ready to leave. I wanted to attend more classes with my new friends. We truly enjoyed each other's company. I had a different life at the hospital, and it seemed a lot simpler and not crazy—no pun intended. For the first time in my life, I felt the freedom of not having any responsibilities other than to myself. I was not ready to face the uncertainty of the outside world or deal with my family again. I was afraid of being scolded by them. I really didn't want to go home, but I was completely wrong. My family was all pleased to hear I was finally coming home.

On a beautiful and warm summer day, I had a follow-up appointment with my psychiatrist. Before I left that morning, my sister-in-law, Julie, called to check on how I was doing. For some reason, she mentioned I should research "Joyce Meyer." I had no idea who she was and cannot recall why Julie recommended her.

After my appointment, I went to a bookstore, found the Joyce Meyer collection, and purchased her CD. When I got into my car, I turned on the CD and fell in love with her Bible teaching. I truly believe Julie's phone call and Joyce's CD were the continuation of God showing me the way.

The following week, God showed me the way back to the bookstore to purchase a Bible. I had never read the Bible and was unaware that there were several versions. The Bible became the light of my life. From that moment on, God has been the light that continues to shine on me. Through His messages, He shows me the right way, and He convicts me when I have gone the wrong way. Every morning, I say a prayer to avoid any temptations toward going the wrong way:

Let the morning bring me word of Your unfailing love for I have put my trust in You. Show me the way I should go, for to You I entrust my life. Rescue from my enemies Lord, for I hide myself in You. (Psalm 143:8–9 NIV)

The Truth

If you abide by My Word, you are truly My disciples and will know the truth and the truth shall set you free.
—John 8:31–32 (ESV)

The truth is I did not understand what the "Word" meant or understand the difference between a book, a chapter, and a verse. I would not have been able to explain the difference between the Old Testament and the New Testament. I had no idea what the four Gospels were. I was completely clueless. Someone gave us a beautiful Bible for a wedding present, but the only time I opened it was to look at the pictures. I had no interest of reading the Bible. I considered the Bible just another religious item that I didn't need since I already had faith, knew how to pray, and attended Mass weekly. *What else do I need?*

The truth is that I was ignorant. After finally purchasing my first Bible, I was very eager to learn the Word, and I was amazed that I was hungry to learn God's Word. My hunger grew each day during the three years it took me to finally finish reading the Bible. I even imagined myself as one of Jesus's disciples. Once I understood that God's Word will provide me the truth, the Bible became the most sacred item I own. It travels with me on my business trips.

Throughout my self-study of the Bible, God opened my eyes to the truth. He also started to show me the plans He has for me. As an example, my mother was a teacher, and I have always had a desire to teach like she did. When I was younger, I volunteered to teach the children's class at church, but I really didn't know what I was doing. After graduating with my MBA, I signed up to be a certified teacher without knowing why I had even signed up. Now, I know why.

The truth is that God wanted me to teach His Word, and I glorify Him every chance I have. Maybe someday I can be an evangelist who preaches the Gospel to a huge crowd of believers. That would be my ultimate dream come true. For now, this book is God's plan for me to share my story and others.

The truth is that you are reading this book because it was God's plan for you.

The Life

> For we live by faith, not by sight.
> —2 Corinthians 5:7 (NIV)

After God showed me the way and the truth, He started to lead me to a new life I had never dreamed was possible. This new life started on April 18, 2014. I was getting ready for work and putting my makeup on in my bathroom. Without warning, Jesus showed me His face; it was as if the reflection on the mirror was His. It probably lasted two seconds, but it was enough time for me to realize what had happened. It was the most unbelievable experience. My husband was talking to me, but I was too numb from what had happened to understand what he was saying. At that moment, I didn't share the experience with my husband because I was afraid of being mocked so I kept it to myself. "Blessed are the pure in heart, for they will see God." (Matthew 5:8 NIV). At that moment, did Jesus show His face to me because I had a pure heart?

Ever since that day, I have been craving a repeat of that moment, but it hasn't happened yet. Do I only have one chance—or was that the only day I had a pure heart? What was Jesus's message to me? In my heart, I believe I know what His message was: "This is how

I want you to be" or "You're doing exactly what I want you to do." Seeking His face became my absolute goal. It is the life I want to live. "You will seek me and find me when you seek me with all your heart" (Jeremiah 29:13 NIV).

My life was changing every day. As a matter of fact, God graced me with an abundant life after I committed myself to Him. What does it mean to have a life in abundance? It means that unexpected things will happen in your life that you can only confidently know came from God. Happy things, peaceful things, and prayers answered. You will experience peace and joy. You will smile more than ever. You will enjoy life.

As for me, unbelievable events started to happen in my life that I know would not have been possible without God. First, my Bible study became successful, and the number of attendees and sessions—including online—increased. Second, I became more fluent with the Gospels' teachings. Third, I became a minister and formed my own ministry: the LIFE (Living in Faith Everyday) Group. Fourth, I was appointed to lead a group at work and was introduced to our CEO—one of my most admired and respected leaders. Fifth, I transferred to a new role and received a promotion instead of being laid off. Lastly and most importantly, my relationship with my family flourished, my temper diminished, and I became more patient and forgiving. My life changed.

The life that I have today is because of the relationship I have with God. I neither worry about nor become consumed with problems. I leave it all to Him. My only objective and ultimate goal is to love Him with all my heart, soul, and mind, and whatever I do, I do to honor and glorify God. The rest of my life is all about Him.

Are you ready for God to show you the Way, the Truth, and the Life?

Theresa: Lead by Example

> See that no one repays another with evil for evil, but always
> seek that which is good for one another and for all people.
> —1 Thessalonians 5:15 (AMP)

Theresa said, "I always wanted to be like Jesus Christ."

Theresa always believed that Jesus is "the Way, the Truth, and the Life," and she demonstrates her belief on a daily basis. She works as a full-time charge nurse at a cancer unit and volunteers at a food bank. While growing up, Theresa learned about faith from her parents. They showed her their faithfulness to God, and Theresa followed her parents' footsteps. Her mother believed in "walking in the path of Jesus."

The Bible teaches us to be like Jesus, and Theresa is dedicated to doing just that. I do not believe I have ever met anyone who has boldly admitted their dedication like Theresa has. While performing her duties as a nurse and a manager leading other nurses, she practices an admirable leadership style of leading by example. She leads by showing how to be good and kind to her cancer patients and the families who are hanging on to their loved ones. The environment she works in might feel like a place where there's a dark cloud hanging over us, but caregivers like Theresa who consistently offer goodness and kindness bring the light to their patients.

"God is love." Theresa displays her love to the poor and the hungry while volunteering at a food bank. It is bothersome to see that we have so many hungry people and homeless people in a country as rich as the United States. Thankfully, we have places like food banks that offer relief to the needy and volunteers like Theresa who serve them. Theresa's display of love reminds me of Jesus feeding the five thousand (Matthew 14:13–21).

Theresa's story is beautiful and inspiring, and I am so blessed to know her.

Theresa said, "If you show people how you live, then maybe they will follow."

In my heart, I believe when God proclaimed, "Let there be light." God created Theresa to be that light and be someone who practices like Jesus so we can all follow.

Emily and Melissa: Pray Big

> But if we are living in the light, as God is in the
> light, then we have fellowship with each other.
> —1 John 1:7 (NLT)

Emily was raised in a Christian family and has two beautiful, good-hearted children. She can easily shine the light on the entire room when she walks in with her contagious smile. Emily follows Jesus and believes He is the way, the truth, and the life through the Holy Spirit.

Emily said, "He's my all, and when a person follows the Holy Spirit, He will lead you to the light."

Psalm 18 teaches us that God will enlighten our darkness and deliver us from our enemies. Emily focuses on the Holy Spirit, knowing He is with her, especially during the really hard times.

"If you stop every day and think and listen to His voice, He will show you the way. Think back in time when He was probably telling you what to do, but you logically ended up doing what you wanted to do."

Emily starts every day with a prayer. A big sign in her bathroom says, "Pray big." Emily prays for everyone—even animals! A few months ago, her girlfriend, Melissa, found her horse in the mud one morning. Melissa was able to get her horse up and took her to the vet. The vet told her that the horse had a twisted gut and most likely would not survive. Melissa called Emily and was very distraught, and Emily told her she would pray for the horse. Emily prayed, knowing it would be "intensely painful" for Melissa if she lost the horse.

Melissa doubted that prayers would work on animals.

Melissa's sister said, "Well, most things Emily prays for work—so we better get busy and start praying too."

The next day, two other vets were called in and provided the same conclusion that the horse needed to be euthanized. Melissa said her goodbyes to the horse and told the vet to just let her know when the procedure had been completed.

The vet prepared for the procedure and walked into the room to begin the process. When he walked in, the horse looked at him with completely clear eyes and whinnied. He stopped and thought, *This is an improvement.* He could not bring himself to continue. He checked later, and the horse was standing and acting normal. Hallelujah! Emily's prayer had been answered! It turned out the vet was also a believer and had never seen anything like it. He believed it had to be divine intervention.

What a beautiful story of the power of prayer—whether the request is big or small, whether it is for a person or animal, and whether the person is a believer or not. Emily felt the heavy burden of her friend, and she prayed big just like the sign in her bathroom.

"For whatever a man sows, this and only this he will reap" (Galatians 6:7 AMP).

Emily planted a good seed by showing the power of prayer—even for animals. She faithfully believes that if "we plant our seeds well, miracles will start to happen."

God is our Deliverer, and He will deliver us from evil. He will deliver us from our enemies, and nothing is impossible with Him, our almighty Savior. He will shine His light on you just like He did for Emily and Melissa. Let us all pray big, be good examples for others, and follow His path—just like Emily does every day.

Vangie: You Light Up my Life

> The light shines in the darkness, and the
> darkness has not overcome it.
> —John 1:5 (NIV)

Vangie, or "Baby Van" as I call her, is an answered prayer of my special devotion to Mama Mary. She is the younger of my adorable twin nieces. Vangie communicates very openly and displays a sharp and inquisitive mind, which is similar to my younger sister, Vangie's mom. At times, when Vangie is less serious, she is very playful, chatty, and fun to be around. My prediction is she will become a very successful lawyer someday, and everyone will want to be represented by her.

Vangie is only eight years old, but she seems older because of the way she speaks and from some of the comments she makes in some of our family conversations. My husband teases and describes her as the "youngest old lady in the world." She knows she will forever be my Baby Van. She enjoys being surrounded by people of all ages, and her presence can light up a room. When she walks in, it feels like a large and bright angel is following her around. Vangie's confident and courageous manner reminds me of Archangel Gabriel, the mightiest and strongest angel. Gabriel means the "might of God."

Vangie loves God and talks with Him through prayer. One of those instances was when my father died. Vangie and my father "Papa" were the best of friends. She loved being carried by him, sung to by him, and fed by him. The two were inseparable, but their time spent together became limited when he became ill and needed to be in a nursing home. Vangie was unable to see him as often as she wanted to, but her heart was always with him. She described his death as a time of "darkness."

Vangie's faith is strong, and she prayed to God to help her come out of this darkness and to see her light, her best friend, her Papa. Shortly after the funeral, while she was on the way home, she claimed that she saw him in the distance. Papa loved walking around as part of his exercise, and she said, "Papa was walking on the sidewalk with a plaid shirt and jeans." During my interview, she wanted me to share that seeing him was an answer to one of her many prayers to God.

Vangie diligently prays and give thanks to God about other matters, including her family, her school, and her soccer games. In the case of Papa's death, she prayed that everyone in our family would believe that just like God is the light of our lives, so is her Papa because he is no longer suffering from his illness.

When I was crying, Vangie said, "I don't want to see you sad."

When you were eight, do you remember praying and giving thanks to God like Vangie does? I can honestly say I was not as close to God as Vangie is at her age.

Today, Vangie focuses on believing that Papa is the light of her life. She longs to be with him and to hear his beautiful voice singing to her again. She is confident God will show her Papa again. Vangie is praying for peace and joy for everyone, and she wants to share a prayer: "I pray for confidence and for all of you to be courageous."

Isn't it admirable that her prayer for all of us is the same manner she walks on to keep Papa in the light?

Vangie's song to Papa is "You Light Up My Life" by Debby Boone:

> You light up my life
> You give me hope to carry on
> You light up my days
> And filled my nights with songs
> It can't be wrong when it feels alright
> Coz you light up my life.

God Is Our Deliverer

> The Lord is my rock, my fortress and my deliverer; My
> God is my rock in whom I take refuge; my shield and the
> horn of my salvation. He is my stronghold, my refuge,
> and my savior from violent people. You save me.
> —2 Samuel 22:2–3

God is the light of the world. Envision yourself walking toward the end of a path to a bright and shiny place where you believe God is. When you walk toward the light, what are you thinking about? How long is the path?

As we go through life, we walk on a path to a light at the end and finally meet Jesus. He is waiting for us, but as we walk down that path, the enemy will do anything possible to block us by having us experience hardships that disrupt our walk or convince us to stop walking (stop believing). Let us not allow the devil to win. Stay focused and believe the light at the end is where God is. That is where you finally meet Jesus.

My father just died, and coincidentally, I am writing about the path. My father walked a long path and lived a life as a loving father, husband, and grandfather. During his walk, he was very faithful to God. My father was my hero, teacher, mentor, and comforter. When he reached the light, he became strong and healthy again. My father is running, biking around, and singing with his beautiful voice to Jesus in heaven. As my heart aches over my father's passing, I am healed in knowing he is now with God. Today, I have two eternal Fathers watching over and guiding me. See you in my dreams, Daddy.

I am excited to continue to walk on my path toward meeting the almighty God. Jesus has shown himself to me, and I look forward to meeting Him again, talking with Him, and continuing to serve Him in heaven. Until then, I will continue to serve the Lord with gladness and faithfulness. I matter to Him—and so do you.

Where are you now? Are you ready to turn on the light for God to show you the Way, the Truth, and the Life?

Do I even Matter? Yes, you do!

> May the Lord bless you and protect you. May the Lord smile on you and be gracious to you. May the Lord show you His favor and give you peace. (Numbers 6:24–26 NLT)

What is the symbol of light for you? Does it mean hope? Does it mean peace? Does it mean it is God?

We all matter to God. His light symbolizes the hope, peace, and joy that only comes from Him. We must turn on the light and welcome Him into our lives. I turned on my light by teaching a Bible study, Theresa turns on her light each time she walks the path of Jesus, Melissa praying big for others is her way of turning on God's light, and Vangie is guided by God's light through her Papa.

May you find and turn on God's light so that you will start to hear His voice in no time!

Do I Even Matter?

Notes from Chapter 3

- What does the symbol of light mean for you?
- Does it mean hope?
- Does it mean peace?
- Does it mean it is God?

CHAPTER 4

Hearing God's voice

Therefore, as the Holy Spirit says, "Today, if you hear His voice,
do not harden your hearts."
—Hebrews 3:78 (ESV)

Can you or have you heard God's voice?
How do you know it is Him?

Do You Hear What I Hear?

I am so thankful that I am now able to
hear God's voice of wisdom, and I talk
with Him all day long. His voice comes
in various ways and is unique for each of

God's
Message
to
Me

us. Some people say they hear a gentle whisper, others feel a nudge,
and some say He speaks to their hearts. It is not an audible voice. It
can be an experience or an answer to a prayer.

Have you ever experienced going into a church service—and
the entire sermon was exactly what you needed? Did it feel like the
pastor was preaching directly at you? I have learned to recognize
when He speaks to me. With His voice, I am where I am today. I

first heard His voice when I found myself responding to someone, but I had absolutely no idea it was Him.

If you have not heard His voice or know how to hear it, the first and most important lesson is to renew your mind.

Renewal of the Mind

My psychiatric counselor, Mary, was a real nice lady with a gentle voice. Mary's office was small, but it had a comfortable couch for our sessions. It was exactly what I envisioned when meeting with a psychiatrist.

The sessions were meant to "help me get back on my feet," but I was already studying God's Word:

> Do not be conformed to this world but be transformed
> by the renewing of the mind. (Romans 12:2)

One of the ways I hear God's voice is through my study. I may be going through something good or bad, and it will coincidentally be the chapter I am studying in the Bible. On the next visit with Mary, I said, "This was our last session. I don't believe a psychiatrist is necessary to help me get back on my feet. I have found God, and He is now my Counselor for life."

Mary understood, but she was adamant that I was making the wrong decision. We closed our session and bid farewell. Do you think I made the wrong decision?

Renewal of the mind needs to become a daily habit. We must apply it to every act and thought we have. It took me a long time to form this habit, and I am still working on it. Renewing your mind is a part of spiritual maturity, and it could take you as long as you live. I believe we become spiritually mature when we meet Jesus in heaven. After renewing your mind, God's voice will become clearer and louder.

Who Is Your BFF?

Growing up, I kept to myself. In grade school and high school, I had one friend for each term. In college, I had none. I was too focused on studying and "didn't need anyone." In grad school, I most definitely didn't need one or have the time for it. When I got married and had children, we already know how that went for me.

Throughout my life, I had acquaintances and felt comfortable at that level. It was difficult to start and maintain close friendships. Talking with people was easy because I was not a shy person, but I had a big trust issue. Selfishly, I used to say, "I don't need friends, and if I had friends, I would have to buy them presents during the holidays." No wonder I found it hard to have friends, I was the Grinch.

When I got saved, God convicted me of my selfishness, taught me the meaning of relationships, and surrounded me with a new set of friends and acquaintances. My new friends are the people I teach Bible study with nationally and globally, the believers at work, the people I recruit from my entire region (nine states), and the people I help at the food bank. God gave me my new job, which has allowed me to engage with people from all walks of life. I have been asked to sit on several boards across the country, which has given me opportunities to extend my network globally. He connected me with all these people—a number I never imagined possible in my life. It was another way where God wants me to have an overflowing and abundant life: "I came that they may have life and have it abundantly" (John 10:10).

Through these relationships, I finally found my true best friend forever. God has become my BFF, and I take every opportunity to introduce and glorify Him around the world. His plan for me was to become His messenger so that when I hear His voice, I will share His messages:

Dawn: The Windmills of your Mind

> The friendship of the Lord is for those who fear
> Him, and he makes known to them His covenant.
> (Psalm 25:14 ESV)

Can God Be Your BFF?

> For to set the mind of the flesh is death, but
> the mind of the Spirit is life and peace.
> —Romans 8:6

Dawn and I met at a restaurant bar. It sounds comical because it sounds like I picked her up at a bar. She was with a coworker, and I was with my husband. We were both savoring our delicious appetizers on a nice relaxing Wednesday afternoon. The restaurant was next to a lake, and when the sun sets, the rays hit the water, which creates a majestic view of the lake.

Our tables were next to each other, but we were both consumed with our own conversations. Based on how Dawn and her friend were dressed, I could tell they were successful businesswomen. As the afternoon went on, Dawn and her friend noticed the white summer shoes I was wearing and gave me a compliment. This sparked a conversation between us, and we immediately connected. We all ended up ordering dinner after our appetizers, and by the end of the evening, I was inviting both to join my Bible study. God planned for Dawn and me to meet at the same place and time. Dawn still attends my Bible study and has become one of my sisters in Christ.

Dawn is a child of God, and she talks with Him throughout the day, especially when she is going through a difficult time. "Okay, God, I know you're there—and you care about the details."

It is such a great practice to talk with God, and it is comforting if you practice it all the time. God wants to be a part of every moment, decision, question, and step of life. He is the almighty God, and absolutely nothing is bigger than Him—not even the biggest or most difficult problems we face. He is our Father, and we are all His children. We look up to Him as a child looks up to a parent while they hold each other's hands. How often do you look up as a child to God?

> Truly I say to you, whoever does not receive the kingdom of God like a child shall not enter it. (Mark 10:15 ESV)

Dawn hears God's voice all the time. He responds to her, and Dawn knows it is Him through "affirmations or coincidences." During our times of trials and tribulations, our minds are heavily consumed with our problems, and they spin like a wheel when we are trying to figure out a solution.

Our problems can hurt us emotionally and physically. They can keep us awake for most of the night as we toss and turn. I became an expert on many sleepless nights. Have you? As such, it can be difficult to hear or feel God's presence when worries take over. That is the work of the enemy (devil). The enemy will persist on destroying our peace and joy (John 10:10) with our problems, and during this time, we must forcefully fight the good fight of faith (1 Timothy 6:12).

Dawn fights the enemy by constantly renewing her mind. "When I am all spun out, I rein myself in, wait, and listen for God."

What do you do to fight the enemy? Maybe we can all follow Dawn's practice of stopping, talking with Him through prayer, waiting, and listening for God. I think of "The Windmills of Your Mind" by Noel Harrison:

> Like a circle in a spiral, like a wheel within a wheel
> Never ending or beginning on an ever-spinning reel
> As the images unwind, like the circles that you find
> In the windmills of your mind.

Dawn is a beautiful lady, and her personality is as beautiful as she is. She is a mother of a very handsome young man, and she has a close relationship with him. Dawn has been divorced twice, and starting a new relationship with another man was not a priority for her—until she met Sam. They enjoyed spending time together, and as time went on, their relationship bloomed.

Unfortunately, their relationship ended tragically when Sam unexpectedly committed suicide. A person survived by someone who has died from suicide will experience extreme emotional distress. A suicide is an unbelievable act that causes mental pain for the people left behind when they try to figure out the cause. It is like putting together a puzzle, but it will never be completed because the missing piece—the person who committed suicide—will never return.

That part of Dawn's life was beyond difficult, but she practiced what she preached. Dawn stopped, prayed, waited, and listened for God. As expected, God's voice manifested through His affirmations—and He used dolphins to comfort Dawn. God does have a sense of humor. Why dolphins?

Dawn said, "Sam liked dolphins. He had a metal statue/tower of a stack of dolphins on a table near his sofa and a glass dolphin in his kitchen. When I see a dolphin, I think of Sam."

Sam doubted many things, including his belief in God, but God must have touched Sam's heart because Sam unexpectedly invited Dawn to church. That was God's way of letting Sam hear His voice. As a believer, Dawn gladly accepted his invitation, and attending Sunday services became a routine for them. Did God touch Sam's heart to prepare him as he entered heaven? I think so.

Shortly after Sam's passing, Dawn prayed and said, "God, is Sam okay?"

God answered her prayers, and a few days later, a bitmoji of dolphins suddenly appeared on her phone. It was an image of two dolphins, and one of them was in the light. A bitmoji is a cartoon app that needs be sent by a person to another person's phone. Dawn had eliminated the app from her phone, and no one admitted to sending it to her. The bitmoji just appeared. For Dawn, it was an affirmation from God to let her know Sam was okay. Other images of dolphins appeared for Dawn as the months went by, and she found so much comfort in knowing Sam went to heaven and is now with our Father.

Dawn's story is threefold. One, a nonbeliever can hear God's voice and transition to becoming a believer. Two, it is a story of how God's love brought two people together. Three, it shows how eternal love will always keep them together. That love may be through images of dolphins, but it is an everlasting affirmation for Dawn that Sam will forever be in her heart.

Have you lost someone you love dearly and felt the same affirmation as Dawn? If not, that is all right. No matter how long it has been since you lost someone, pray to God and ask Him—just like Dawn did. You will hear His voice when He speaks to your heart via a feeling, a coincidence, or an affirmation. Only you will know when it is Him. It is the most wonderful feeling in the world.

Merilee: Everything Happens for a Reason

> For everything there is a season, a time
> for every activity under heaven.
> —Ecclesiastes 3:21 (NLT)

Do you believe things happen for a reason? Do you think God's answer is sometimes different than what you wanted? It is always better.

Merilee and I attended the same high school. If you compare her high school pictures with her pictures today, she still looks as lovely, and she does not appear to have aged at all. In high school, she had short, curly, loose blonde curls, which is similar to the hairstyle she maintains today. Merilee married her high school sweetheart, Kevin—one of the star players of our football team—and they are still happily married. Their love for each other is strong, and they will remain sweethearts forever.

During high school, Merilee and I had some classes together, but the one class I remember fondly was Spanish. Our teacher, Senora Majors, preferred to have quiet students like Merilee, and she frowned on talkative students like me. Merilee had a lot of friends at school, and I had one. She had a boyfriend, and I did not. She attended the school games and school dances, and I was not allowed to. She lived in the north end of Seattle, and I lived in the south. We were total opposites socially and physically.

Thirty years later, our amazing God brought us together through social media. As it turns out, Merilee and I are not opposites after all. We share a common bond emotionally and spiritually. We both have a profound faith in God, and we pray for and with each together. As an introvert, Merilee is inclined to be the quieter and more reserved in group gatherings. Her shyness makes her a better listener, and it is during those moments that she hears and feels God's presence. Merilee said, "God is my companion. He'll help me find the peace."

I also hear and feel God's presence when I quiet myself down. Merilee is a perfectionist, and so am I. We have both been married for thirty years and have two children: a boy and a girl. We now live in the same neighborhood. We are both children of God. Coincidence? No, these are all God's amazing works, according to His own timing.

Everything happens for a reason. Some are good—like my reunion with Merilee—and some are not as good. Merilee's husband has a long history of kidney problems, and even after two successful operations, he still required a transplant. It was a long time of uncertainty and unsettling period while their family waited for a kidney that would work for Kevin. Fortunately, a family member's kidney was found to be a perfect match, and the transplant was successful. Most of us have experienced uncertainty like that, and the feelings are unsettling. During those moments, we must quiet ourselves down and listen to hear God's voice.

Merilee said, "God doesn't let you go through rough waters."

The high school sweethearts sold their house and moved to a condo with a romantic view of the water. Maintenance was less expensive, and the location was great. They felt like they had made the wrong decision to move, but Merilee's strong faith reminded her to practice "to look forward and not look back." She also believed the move happened for a reason—just like Kevin's medical condition—and she was right. Her son lived with them at the condo, and just like Merilee, Scott was shy and quiet. The condo environment challenged Scott's introverted personality and pushed him to engage with other people in the complex. As a result, Scott blossomed and gained more confidence in meeting other people.

Everything happened for a reason for Merilee. The sweethearts eventually sold their condo and purchased another home. Scott moved out and is living in his own apartment. Kevin is relieved of his kidney problems, and they now spend time traveling around in their motor home. Merilee and Kevin will remain sweethearts forever.

Jamie: Love at First Sight

> Let all that you do be done in love.
> —1 Corinthians 16:14 ESV

The National Shrine of Our Mother of Perpetual Help (Baclaran Church) is in the northern part of Manila. Many devoted Catholics flood this enormous church every day to visit her shrine and attend special devotional masses every Wednesday. As one of the largest churches in the Philippines, it has a full seating capacity of two thousand, but as many as eleven thousand people stand wall to wall to fit inside, especially during Mass on Wednesdays. Some people stand outside and around the church just to hear Mass via the loudspeakers. This enormous church is mostly made of concrete, and it stands very tall with high open ceilings. All the doors and windows remain open to allow for the breeze to come in. When you walk in, crowded or not, a sense of peace and feeling of hope comes from within. It is the most amazing feeling.

I learned to become devoted to our Mama Mary, and I learned to plow through an extremely crowded church from my own mother. During one of our trips back home, I visited the shrine with my parents and prayed for two very special devotions. To show your devotion and ask for a special petition to Mama Mary, one must walk on bended knees on concrete floor from the very back of the church all the way to the front of the church where the shrine is located. The distance between the back to the front was about 350 feet. I successfully completed my walk on bended knees, reached the shrine with very bruised knees, got up very slowly, and with a smile on my face, turned back to find my mother to let her know I had made it. It was a significant moment to be able touch the shrine and whisper my special devotional prayer to Mama Mary.

A month later, Mama Mary answered my prayer when I received a call from my brother-in-law.

He said, "They are due to come in November."

"What? What do you mean by *they*?"

Nine months later, on a cold November evening, my sister was blessed with giving birth to two beautiful twin daughters. I can still recall the first time I saw my Jamie. The tiny human being on my sister's left arm opened her little eyes and looked at me. It was love at first sight.

Today, Jamie is an eight-year-old second grader at Saint Anthony School. She is a very sweet girl—super smart just like my sister— and she loves to write. At such a young age, Jamie has become an inspiration for me. She has written me letters, short stories, and even a prayer. She shared a prayer from school that we can both say the next time she comes over my house, but I pray it every morning before I begin writing.

Jamie hears God's voice in many ways. She said, "He made

Jesus, makes miracles happen, and gave us the Holy Spirit." She also talks to God every night through a prayer. "When I'm not happy, I ask God to make it work for me—and I am still thankful even if it doesn't work."

Jamie's response filled my heart with joy, and I was intrigued by her strong beliefs. Jamie prays when she is frustrated.

How can someone so young be frustrated at anything? As her aunt, I am cautiously protective, and my heart ached when I heard she was experiencing frustration.

Jamie explained that she feels frustrated when she cannot solve a very hard math problem.

Aha! That answer gave me a lot of comfort. Thankfully, it was a math problem that caused her frustration. I love math and would be frustrated also if I could not solve a problem.

Jamie is a very loving and wonderful big sister to her twin Vangie. Jamie shows her love to God by loving Him and loving others. Aren't those the two most important commandments? At the conclusion of our interview, my heart melted when she shared a special prayer for all my readers: "For God to help someone or something through me."

I love my Jamie so much, and our love was truly love at first sight.

God Is Our Counselor

> But the Advocate, the Holy Spirit, whom the Father
> will send in my name, will teach you all things and
> will you of everything I have said to you.
> —John 14:16 NIV

Almost every day, we make decisions about what to do or say. The challenge is when we must make hard decisions that could affect our families, our health, our families' health, our finances, or our jobs. A normal reaction is to seek advice from a parent, spouse, best friend, doctor, mentor, or priest or minister.

The Bible teaches us that God is our Counselor—and we should seek Him first. I am not saying we should disregard the advice of close family members and friends because it is important to hear, especially from parents. However, "for the Lord your God in your midst is a jealous God" (Deuteronomy 6:15 ESV), and He wants to be a part of everything we do. That means everything and every moment.

Do I even matter? Yes, you do!

> O Lord hear me as I pray; pay attention to my groaning. Listen to my cry for help, my King, and my God, for I pray to no one but you. Listen to my voice in the morning, Lord. Each morning I bring my requests to you and wait expectantly. (Psalm 5:1–3 NLT)

We all matter to God, and He lets us hear His voice in many ways. We can hear His voice with our thoughts and in our hearts, through affirmations, coincidences, events, songs, or even images such as dolphins. Renewing our minds is the beginning of spiritual maturity, and it is an ongoing cycle until we meet God. For now, enjoy your life while He speaks to you in a way that only you can know it is Him!

Notes from Chapter 4

- Have you heard God's voice?
- How did you know it was Him?

CHAPTER 5

I Am God's Messenger

Whatever you do, do your work heartily, as for the Lord rather
than for men knowing that from the Lord you will receive the
reward of the inheritance. It is the Lord Christ whom you serve.
—Colossians 3:23–24 (NASB)

What do you think God's purpose is for your life? What do you
think God has asked you to do?

A Servant's Heart

I listened to an interview with one of our organization's senior
executives. Ed was asked what books he reads. Just like the person
who asked the question, I was keen to hear his response because the
types of books we read can reveal our character.

Ed explained that his number one "go-to" book was the Bible.
Yes! He is a believer and comfortably shares his faith.

After the call, I sent him an email to let him know we shared
the same "go-to" book.

He responded, "Colossians 3:23–24."

Once again, God's amazing timing shined. I was writing this
section and was at a loss for words, and He just gave me the gift of

wisdom and guided me toward what message to share. I was pleased with the connection.

However, Ed's response sparked reactions from some of my team members, and based on their comments, I was able to discern the believers versus the nonbelievers. Ed's response was criticized and labeled as a "land mine" that could cause an "unwarranted judgment against us."

I found myself becoming angrier as I read the email, but God reminded me of James 1:19:

> Understand this brethren, be quick to hear, slow to speak, slow to take offense and slow to anger, for a man's anger does not serve the righteousness of God.

I refrained from responding to their comments. Instead, I reminded myself that a nonbeliever does not have a servant's heart for God. It is who they are. It describes their character. How can we help them believe? Can you be God's messenger for a nonbeliever?

Since you are reading this book and have made it this far, I am confident you share the same servant's heart as Ed and me. Most importantly, God is pleased and smiling at all of us, knowing our hearts belong to Him. In our servant's hearts, we will find the true treasure that only God can provide. It is the treasure of love, peace, and joy that I long for. Do you long for the same treasure as I do?

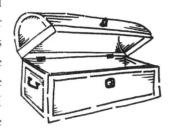

An Abundant Life

With God, nothing is impossible. Whatever we are experiencing, we will come out of it in accordance with God's will. The Bible teaches us that He will set us up way above our expectations and we are to live abundantly until it overflows. Some of you may have doubts about the thought of living abundantly. How is that even possible? I am evidence of the possibility. Let me share my experience with you.

The year 2014 marked the onset of my abundant life with God. Most of the pastors and priests obtained several years of formal education to be "officially ordained" in their profession. In June of that year, I was "officially ordained" online as a minister by filling out a form without years of formal education. To tell you the truth, I thought it was silly. It felt fake, but God put it in my heart—and I obeyed. At least I had learned not to ask, "Why me, God?" Instead, I felt a driving force and a mental strength that I cannot explain. I was confident that the strength would only come from the grace of our almighty God. I was absorbed with passion and commitment to solely focus on following His lead.

In three years, I successfully completed my formal education with God as my teacher. I completed reading and studying the Bible from front to back, and the result was more than five hundred notecards of scriptures that I desired to memorize (see Appendix D). It was also during this time that my Bible study launched, and I began connecting with an increasing flow of believers. My obedience and relationship with Him were in complete alignment with the abundant peace and joy I was experiencing. As God's messenger, the more I shared His Word, the more my life got better. I didn't worry about anything, and nothing bothered me. My life was filled with abundant joy and peace.

At the end on 2016, God blessed me with an opportunity to lead an employee network for my company. His blessing came with the same passion and commitment I had two years prior, but this time, the passion and commitment was for helping others. I had no idea how to start or even lead a network, but He blessed me with the wisdom and strength to do it. Just like my Bible study, there was an increasing flow of connections. This time, it was with my colleagues in our organization, which are up to 968, and can increase much higher since our network just launched globally. Are you able to see what is happening here? God is executing His plan, and I need to follow His lead. The more I share His Word, obey Him, and glorify Him, the more blessings He provides for me. It just goes hand in hand. It is that simple.

In 2017, I faced a layoff situation and was confused because suddenly—during my abundant life—I was faced with a negative situation. It did not make sense to me at the time, but through my studies, I have learned not to worry or doubt. I graciously followed His lead again, but I felt some hesitation since I was not yet spiritually mature.

Was God testing my patience, the one character I struggled with the most? Oh, yes, He was. God knew I had grown weary with my current work, and He took me away from a situation I could no longer endure and blessed me with an opportunity to move to a different role within my company. God is faithful, and He will always find a way out.

My new role allowed for working remotely and some travel. God knew I loved traveling, and He also knew that my schedule would need some flexibility. Why? My father was diagnosed with dementia in 2018. With my ability to work remotely, I was able to fulfill my work responsibilities at my parents' home, accompany them to their medical appointments or other errands, and keep an eye on them. God wanted me to be there as I monitored my father's declining health. However, regardless of what has happening with my father, I still felt like I was living abundantly and cherishing the moments with my father until he died peacefully in 2020. God was in control. No questions asked.

As I write this section, our current environment is filled with fear due to the pandemic and racial issues and questions. There is a heightened uncertainty about jobs and the well-being of this great country. I am not afraid of contracting the illness or being a target of racial discrimination, and it is not because I am arrogant. The color of my skin should not identify who I am; my godly character is what defines me. That is God's message that I need to send out. The means to send out His message is never clear until it happens. God just comes out of nowhere, leads me to execute His plan for me, and rewards me with a blessing. There are times when I feel that His abundant grace is overflowing, and then He surprises me again with something new and spectacular. God is in control, and He always has a better plan.

God is truly amazing, and if you trust Him wholeheartedly, cling to Him, glorify Him, and love Him with all your heart, soul, and mind, you will experience an overflowing abundant life with peace, joy, dreams, thoughts, and hope that will leave you in awe over and over again.

My work for God is to be His messenger. What do you think God has asked you to do? You must have some idea about what it is. Be fearless and go for it. God is in control!

Tracy: A Chance to Give Back

> Give, and it will be given to you.
> —Luke 6:38 (AMP)

Every evening, I check my calendar to review the meetings I have scheduled for the next day. For a meeting to be efficient and effective, a structured agenda must be established. Somehow, I had a meeting with a lady named Tracy without an agenda. It was simply titled "Introductions." Unlike all my meetings, I felt unprepared because it didn't have an agenda—or at least I thought it didn't. God had an agenda.

Tracy was a lovely young professional who has been employed

with our company for a couple of years. She works for our marketing department, and she requested a call to learn more about my experience and career path. Her interest was based on her own desire to follow my path and someday reach the point where I am in my career today. I never thought anyone would be interested in knowing my path. What an honor to be asked!

Our discussion involved my education, experience, the steps I followed, and how fortunate I was to have found great mentors. Most importantly, I shared the lessons I learned from my mistakes, which I used to hide. At the end of our call, she felt like she could follow a good path forward. We didn't share our beliefs during the call.

Tracy sent a follow-up email to express her gratitude and closed her note with a scripture. Bingo! I figured out why Tracy was on my schedule without an agenda; it was not our agenda that we needed to discuss. We needed to follow God's agenda, which was to discuss the path He wants her to follow and not mine. Today, Tracy and I connect frequently—and God is always the center of our conversation. As a disciple of God, I don't always have to share His messages. Sometimes He just wants me to be a good listener.

I am honored to have become Tracy's unofficial mentor, and I feel blessed that God gave me a chance to give back by being able to help Tracy—just like my mentors helped me. The Bible became our reference point for next steps.

Tracy's story may be simple and ordinary, but it is very impactful. To be God's messenger does not have to be elaborate or be heard by a lot of people. It can just be a connection between you and whoever God places in front of you. God provides us a chance to give back, and sometimes He just comes out of nowhere and presents you with a stranger.

Who have you met recently? Do you feel like God placed them there for a reason?

Sherryl: Love Is All Around

> And we know that all things work together for good to those who
> love God, to those who are the called according to His purpose.
> —Romans 8:28 (NKJV)

Sherryl was separated from her siblings. A longtime cigarette smoker, she became addicted to drugs, was stricken with lung cancer, was laid off from work, had to move to a different city, and lost a loved one to cancer. However, because of her love for Jesus, Sherryl never gave up. She survived through it all.

There were six children (a boy and five girls) in her family, and when Sherryl was five years old, her parents divorced. Three of her siblings moved to a different state with her father, and the other three, including Sherryl, stayed with her mother. Sherryl adorably speaks about her four other sisters in numbers—sister 1, sister 2, sister 3, and sister 4—and Sherryl is sister 5. It was difficult being apart from her siblings, and writing letters was their only way of communicating. Her biological father did not put forth the effort to connect with her, and Sherryl grew up with her mother, her stepfather, sister 4, and sister 6.

During her teenage years, Sherryl wanted more connection with her siblings who were staying with her father. She wanted more than just writing letters. Sherryl wanted all her siblings to be close together in their hearts—even if they were forced to be physically apart. She wanted all of them to love each other and experience the same love she has for Jesus, which she did not even know she had at such a young age. Sherryl persisted through the years, and today—even after the passing of sister 2 and sister 3, they are still in touch with each other. They experienced some disputes along the way, but isn't that just part of sibling life?

Sherryl smoked cigarettes for a long time. It is a bad and tough habit to quit. I have relatives who have been trying to quit for years and have been unsuccessful. Sherryl also started using drugs for about six months. Thankfully, she was able to end her addiction when she realized it was getting worse. During that time, God was not the center of Sherryl's life. She believed in Him, but she did not have a relationship with Him. Her stepfather encouraged Sherryl and her sisters to believe in God, but there was "no need" to go to church—and reading the Bible was not essential.

God had His plans for Sherryl. He placed in her heart the desire to find a church—even though she was raised believing church was not necessary. Sherryl tried different churches and listened to different pastors. After several attempts, a friend invited Sherryl to her church, and she finally found the right church to worship in—and she found God. It was the beginning of her relationship with Him. She accepted God as her Savior and was later baptized in water. When Sherryl became a believer, God became the center of her life. She said, "God really revealed himself to me." Sherryl prayed for God to help her quit her longtime habit of smoking, and He answered her prayer. Amazing!

Eight months later, God tested Sherryl's faith—and she was diagnosed with stage 2 lung cancer. When we become believers, we will still experience trials and tribulations. Our problems do not go away, but how we face them is different. God is interested in seeing how we behave. Are we going to trust Him completely this time around? Will we obey and be patient as we patiently wait for Him to put our lives back together?

Sherryl required treatment—just like any other cancer patient would—and the cost was expensive. There was even a question of how much her insurance company would pay. It was the last thing she needed to worry about, but she made a heartfelt prayer to God. "Okay, God, you said all things are possible through you. So, here you go—you figure this out."

And He did. Sherryl's prayer was answered again, and miraculously, there was something unique about her cancer. It became research, and her entire bill was removed. Most importantly,

Sherryl's cancer was also removed. The surgeon, also a believer, said her surgery was effortless, and it had to be God's miracle.

God tested Sherryl again when she was laid off from her work during a time when work was hard to find. Sherryl's faith was strong, and she did not worry one bit about unemployment. Because of her faith, belief, and trust in God, she found a great job really quickly.

After the passing of her two oldest sisters, she started missing her family who still lived in the area where she grew up. Even though she had a great job and hated giving it up, she prayed to God to help her one more time. Once again, she put her trust in God.

After she moved, she reconnected with one of her cousins, Wesley. A few months later, Wesley was also diagnosed with lung cancer. Sherryl was by his side to love and comfort him throughout the treatment process. Wesley told Sherryl that he did not have a relationship with God—but he wanted one. Sherryl took Wesley to church and was celebrating with him when he was baptized in water. Wesley was not fortunate enough to be healed from the cancer, and he died. Sherryl was able to help Wesley get the relationship with God he always wanted and find peace before he died. Sherryl also had the honor of delivering the eulogy.

Before Sherryl became a believer, she described herself as a mean-spirited person. "I was not a good person."

I chuckled when she said this because I had thought the same thing about myself. We agreed God had given us both a chance to be a better person. When God started to reveal His love for Sherryl, all she wanted to do was give that love back to others. "Love is what truly matters. I always try to be there for others—to let them know they have someone."

Sherryl is a messenger of God, and I am blessed that He placed her in my life. God planned for her to go through the trials and tribulations she experienced since she was five years old—only to share His message with you through this book. He wants to show that nothing is impossible if you believe in Him.

You are a messenger of God. The next step is deciding how you're going to share your message to others. What do you think God's message has been for you in your life? Can you be like Sherryl and share the love and message He has provided you?

God Is Our Rewarder

> But without faith, it is impossible to please Him, for whoever comes near to God must believe that God exists and that He rewards those seek Him.
> —Hebrews 11:6 (AMP)

While on earth, we all have different jobs. There are jobs that we are compensated for so we can pay our bills and/or save money, and other jobs are voluntary like working at church or food bank. Other jobs include taking care of family as a parent, a sibling, or a good friend. When you think about your current job or jobs you have had in the past—compensated or not—which one did you find the most rewarding? How do you define rewarding?

I have a unique job at work that I am compensated for. I love what I do—not because I get a lot of money—but because I believe the work that I do today is work I do for God and not for humanity. I am God's messenger at whatever I do. Every day, I ask myself, *What is God asking me to do today? Who is He going to place on my schedule that I need to send or share His message with? What will He ask me to do so I can glorify Him?*

My definition of rewarding is when I am able to bring joy to the Lord: "For the joy of the Lord is my strength" (Nehemiah 8:10 NLT). No matter what I am going through, no matter where I am, no matter our financial situation, the comfort of knowing that everything I do will bring joy to Him is all that matters. Nothing else matters.

I shared that writing was my weakness—but look what happened. I am writing away and will complete my first book soon!

This book is my gift to God and my way of glorifying Him with all the wonderful and amazing things He has done repeatedly to me and others. This book may not become a *New York Times* best seller, but I know in my heart that the ultimate reader will be God. He will be the judge, and I cannot wait to see His reward for me!

Do I even matter? Yes, you do!

> Show me your ways, O Lord; Teach me your paths.
> Guide me in your truth and teach me, for you are
> God my savior and my hope is in you all day long.
> (Psalm 25:4–5 NIV)

We all matter to God. We are all His messengers, and He wants you to be His disciple. He wants you to share His Word and His love for you. God wants to reward you with the abundant life that we crave—not with money but with the peace, joy, and love that only He can provide. God will show us the way and guide us along. We just need to trust and follow His lead.

If you are at a loss for words about how or what message to share, please look at appendix C. This is my short version of the book of Proverbs, which I use for my own meditation to help me become who God wants me to be. It has many practical messages that you can use for your own mediations or share with others. I guarantee God will connect you with someone who needs it. Open your heart and hear His voice!

Do I Even Matter?

Notes from Chapter 5

- What is God's purpose for your life?
- What has God asked you to do?

CHAPTER 6

Live in Faith Everyday

He said, "Listen to my words: 'When there is a
prophet among you, I, the Lord, reveal myself to
them in visions, I speak to them in dreams.'"
—Numbers 12:6 (NIV)

Do you believe that all things are possible with God? Are you patient
and eager to see what He has in store for you?

To Dream the Impossible Dream

My father had the most beautiful voice. He frequently sang to me,
my siblings, and his four grandchildren from the time we were born
until he peacefully died at the age of eighty-seven in February 2020.
When he sang, my father's angelic voice captured everyone around
him, especially me. One of my favorite songs he sang was Andy
Williams's "The Impossible Dream."

We all have dreams, and I believe dreams can come true only if
they truly serve God's purpose or are part of His plan for you. My
previous dreams were materialistic—to be extremely rich so I could
afford anything I want to purchase or have a big title at work—but
my dreams changed drastically after I got saved. Today, and in the

future, my dreams will forever have a common theme: Will my dream glorify God? If yes, then I am confident it will come true because nothing is impossible with Him.

Just like everything else, the timing of my dreams is all in His hands. The main key is to be extremely patient. The thought of this puts a smile on my face because I used to be very impatient, and through God's convictions, I finally learned how to be more patient.

When I was a little girl, I would eagerly and impatiently wait for my father to come home from work to see what surprise he had for me. The Bible teaches us to act like a child and wait expectantly for God:

> And he said: "Truly I tell you, unless you change
> and become like little children, you will never enter
> the kingdom of heaven." (Matthew 18:3 NIV)

While I wait patiently and expectantly for my dreams to come true, I will love Him with all my heart, with all my soul, and with all my mind.

How Do I Love Thee?

This is probably the most important section of my book, and it is worth a bookmark. If there is one scripture I can ask or even beg for you to remember, it is this:

> You shall love the Lord your God with all your
> heart and with all your soul and with all your mind.
> That is the great and first commandment. (Matthew
> 22:37 ESV)

I pray that the table below helps you understand the three components of the loving God.

Heart	Soul	Mind
Emotional: It is how we feel.	Spiritual: It is how we connect with God.	Rational: It is how we think and reason.
Subjective: It makes sense to me.	It is who we are inside.	Objective: It is factual.
The seat of physical life	The deepest aspect of being a person	Brain: Understanding and intelligence
What motivates us	The life force in all of us	Projection of your soul

Every moment of my life today—and forever—evolves around this scripture. Finally learning and understanding that the most important aspect of my life that was missing was my relationship with God is beyond conviction. This most important lesson made me the believer and minister that I am today. It is who I want to be forever. They are the components of my life, my love, and my dreams for God.

How do you love God? What are your dreams?

Ann: In Survival Mode

> I sought the Lord, and He answered me;
> He delivered me from all my fears.
> —Psalm 34:4 NIV

Ann is the loving mom of four beautiful children. When her marriage ended, she felt like it was the end, especially when finances became tight as a single mom raising a young family. Ann is a devout Catholic, and her love for God remained strong even during what felt like a really tough time for her and her children. After you hear her story, you will be amazed by her survival, courage and strength.

Long after her divorce, Ann met a man named John, and she loved him very much. Her children adored him, spent time with him, and respected him as a father. Family time became a norm in Ann's home, and beautiful memories were made. One of their fond memories was a family adventure to visit the ice caves on a beautiful sunny day. It was a place that attracted a lot of visitors from everywhere. At the end of the tour, Ann and her family were having a picnic and enjoying their lunch—sharing thoughts about the beauty of Mother Nature—when tragedy struck.

They heard ice crack and then a scream. About two hundred feet away, a big chunk of ice had hit a little girl named Grace and her mom. Ann and John frantically ran to try to save Grace, but she was pronounced dead when the first responders reached them. It was a horrific experience that affected them both. John fell into severe depression and started to medicate himself with prescription drugs and alcohol. Unfortunately, it reached a point where Ann made the decision to end their relationship to prevent her children from seeing what he had become—and then John did the unthinkable. He committed suicide on Grace's birthday. John's death took a heavy toll on Ann's entire family for a long period of time—until he showed up in their dreams. They saw how peaceful he was with Grace by his side.

While the deaths of Grace and John were so sudden, tragic, and horrible, a believer can see the beauty of both in heaven—even in their dreams. Ann was left with a very empty heart, lost without her love, and had to find the courage to move on. She was back in survival mode.

Ann said, "Beauty comes out of pain. It was during this time God showed me in the most beautiful ways I've ever experienced that He is so very close to us in our lowest most painful times."

One morning, God showed His beautiful presence to Ann. She had the urge to grab a pen and paper, and she started writing. The result was a beautiful poem. "I don't write poetry—never have. The words just came tumbling out. I did not write this poem; it came from above." Grace's family published a book with her poem in it:

Do I Even Matter?

I walked to the top of a mountain one day,
In search of the natural beauty and wonders of this earth abound.
As I walked this path with my loved ones around,
I never anticipated that God's plan for me
that day would be so profound.

The tragedy unfolded, family and strangers all around
Watched as the big snowball came down.
We tried to help her with growing despair, this
little girl who had flown in the air,
Now lay before me on the ground,
Life seemed so unfair.

We worked while we waited for help to arrive,
Then we heard her take that last sigh.
I watched as God held out his hand and said,
"Come with me to the Promised Land."
One life on earth ended, and a new one began.
I sat there crying, chilled to the bone,
As I watched while God guided her to His heavenly home.

Our hearts were filled with great pain
as we began our descent back
Down the mountain that night.
I looked up to the heavens, imagined her
surrounded by great white light,
And heard her say, "I will see you again."

The heavens were rejoicing us, they welcomed her home
But those of us here on earth were left feeling so alone.
Grace, sweet Grace, six months ago today.

Ann survived John and Grace's deaths through her poem. She knows it may take a long time to fully recover, but she is surviving and recovering every day. She hopes to meet another husband, but it hasn't happened yet. "If it is in God's will, it will happen; otherwise, it won't." Sometimes it is hard to see if God is working for us, but when He shows up, it is a wonderful feeling—just like when He showed up for Ann to write the poem.

Ann was financially strapped, and the roof of her house was completely damaged. The estimated cost to repair it was thirty thousand dollars. Was this another "end" she had to battle with? No. While on survival mode, her faith remained strong. Ann prayed for a miracle because there was no way she could afford to pay for the roof. Her neighbor showed up and reminded her that she could probably file a claim with her insurance company to pay for the roof. It was a very slim chance, but it was worth a try. It rains a lot in Seattle, and Ann was biting her teeth while waiting for the insurance company's answer. She was also praying hard that it would not rain. Ann's insurance company approved the claim and fixed the roof, and the next day, it rained heavily! Ann had survived another event.

One of Ann's daughters wanted freedom and decided to explore the world. She made a bold move to pack up and take a trip to other countries. Ann's daughter was filled with excitement, but Ann was filled with fear. Once again, Ann needed to switch to survival mode. The inability to connect with her daughter or know her whereabouts was another grueling situation she had to endure.

After many sleepless nights, God answered Ann's prayers. Her beautiful daughter returned and surprised Ann when she walked into the kitchen. Her arrival was perfect and a real blessing. A week delay would have caused her daughter to be stranded and unable to come home due to the coronavirus pandemic travel limitations. It was an eye-opening lesson for her daughter because her friends who decided to stay were unable to come home. Ann had survived another event.

Ann said, "God showed me in many ways He was there for me, but sometimes I fail to see it." It is not just Ann that fails to see God. I have—and you may have too. Our vision of the truth, which is

God's love, becomes blurry. It feels like our eyes are filled with tears. Our emotions take over, and that makes us physically weaker. We need to remind ourselves of 2 Corinthians 12:9. His strength and power are made perfect and will show themselves when we are weak. God will never leave us or forsake us.

How courageous will you be if tragedy happens to you or your family? Will your faith remain strong if you're in survival mode?

Mr. T: Live Life with Encouraging Moments

> So encourage each to other and build each
> other up just as you are already doing.
> —1 Thessalonians 5:11 (NLT)

Mr. T is a young man who lives in Dallas. We became connected through an employee network group, and I became his unofficial mentor. We later found out we share the same faith and love for God. Mr. T once told me I have helped and encouraged him. On the contrary, I am encouraged by Him.

Wow #1

"Footprints in the Sand" is a popular poem that resonates to Christians. I learned this heartwarming and loving poem when I was in high school many moons ago. An hour before my interview with Mr. T, someone else reminded me of the same poem. At the beginning of my interview with Mr. T, he asked if I was familiar with the poem. Wow! Was it a coincidence that I was reminded of this poem on the exact same day—or was it God's amazingly perfect timing? I say it was the latter.

Wow #2

Mr. T and I met three years ago at a dinner event with four other people. We were discussing an issue that we had to solve.

Mr. T said, "Let's pray about it."

Wow! He believes in praying! My heart beamed with gladness, and I thanked God for the moment. That was the evening I started my connection with Mr. T. We got to know each other through the network we both belonged to, and he has asked me for career advice. Through our faith, we became friends. He said, "God wants to answer prayers, and when we pray and rely on Him, we can see how God will work."

I strongly believe in prayers, and I live in faith every day by talking with God as if He is next to me. God places special people in our lives to help us grow in faith, and He does it in ways that we might never think were possible.

Wow #3

When I asked Mr. T if he believes that all things are possible with God, he shared a scripture that provides strength for him:

I can do anything I need to do in life through Christ who strengthens me. (Philippians 4:13)

Wow! We like the same scripture. Philippians 4:13 is one of my all-time favorite scriptures.

Mr. T said, "It really gives me hope and peace of mind, especially during tough times. My personal perspective is that my current position is just a small moment in the big picture, and God is working through each moment. Sometimes it's hard to see how He is working until after that moment passes."

Mr. T lives in faith every day through his reliance on God. We all have problems—some are big, and some are small—but when the enemy gets a strong hold of us, the enemy covers our eyes. We are blinded by not knowing the truth. God is love, and that is the ultimate truth. It's easy to focus on the problem that seems more apparent. Sometimes it's in hindsight that we see how much God loves us.

Wow #4

I was so fascinated when I learned about our similarities, especially when I found out we share the same weakness. Mr. T is a very talented young man with aspirations of moving up in the corporate world. When I was his age, I had the same aspiration. He struggles with being impatient and the need for instant gratification, but God taught him how to be humble. I was very impatient, and when God taught me humility, it was a very hard lesson.

We both believe all things are possible with God. I encountered these four "Wow" stories with Mr. T, and I can conclude it was not just a coincidence. God made it possible for us to connect even though we live in different states and are very different in age, ethnicity, and gender. We are on two different career paths. Our commonality is our love for God—and He made it possible for us to connect and encourage each other.

Have you been encouraged by someone? Can you help build others and provide the same encouragement?

God Is Our Protector

> The Lord is my protector, He is my strong fortress. My
> God is my protection and with Him I am safe. He protects
> me like a shield. He defends me and keeps me safe.
> —Psalm 18:2

Spiritual maturity starts when someone is saved and becomes a believer. It will take a long time before we are spiritually matured. At fifty, when I thought I was physically mature, I became a believer—and then I had to learn about becoming spiritually mature. It was an amazing turning point for me, and I pray that He will grace me with fifty more years to learn and mature spiritually. I will still make mistakes, but if I focus on having a servant's heart to glorify God, I am confident that He will always be my Protector who will never leave me or forsake me.

Once again, God's timing is perfectly amazing. I wanted to start writing this section today, and God perfectly timed the success of yesterday's work event to write about. Professionally and personally, with all my heart, I just want to help whenever I can. Professionally, I can help by becoming a mentor for someone, help a person find a job within our company, or connect a person with someone else who may be able to help. Yesterday, I coordinated a virtual meeting for the members of the network I lead. There was no agenda. The goal was to simply say hello, to see their beautiful faces, and to find out how everyone was doing during the difficult time of a pandemic crisis. It was an opportunity to think about other people and not just myself.

The event included the CEO of our company, a leader I really admire and respect. He always says, "People are our best asset." If I did not know him, I would say those are just words from a top-ranking person, but I am fortunate to know him and want others to see his authenticity. This is a CEO of an organization with a hundred thousand employees and a pandemic crisis on his mind, but he graciously spent ten minutes of his evening to jump on a virtual call with 150 of his employees just to say hello. How can anyone not be encouraged by him?

I am encouraged by the CEO of my organization, Mr. T, and my colleagues I am connected with. God made it possible to connect with all these people—a connection I never dreamed was possible.

Do I even matter? Yes, you do!

> So as to walk in the manner worthy of the Lord, fully pleasing to Him: bearing good fruit in every good work and increasing in the knowledge of God being strengthened with all power, according to His glorious might, for all endurance and patience with joy. (Colossians 1:10 ESV)

We all matter to God, and He will make your impossible dreams come true. He will place and connect you with people who will make a difference in your life. He will bless you with other believers—your brothers and sisters through Christ—in your neighborhood, at work, and even around the world, just as He has for me. I dreamed an impossible dream, and God made it possible. Go ahead and dream the impossible dream!

Notes from Chapter 6

- Do you believe that with God all things are possible?
- Are you patient and eager to see what He has in store for you?

CHAPTER 7

Leaving a Legacy

So then, each of us will give an account of ourselves to God.
—Romans 14:12 (NIV)

Have you made any travel plans lately? Where were you planning to go?

Leaving on a Jet Plane

My husband and I have enjoyed traveling together since we met thirty-two years ago. Every May, we take a trip to celebrate his birthday and our wedding anniversary. During the summer months, we frequently take short trips by car or ferry to celebrate the weekend. He enjoys long drives while listening to his music, and I enjoy taking a peaceful nap while he drives. We are perfect travel companions. As we plan for our retirement in a few years, we are diligently saving money and are excited to travel more than ever. These are my current travel plans—or are they?

I travel quite a bit with my current job, but it was not until I started writing this chapter that I realized I have been traveling all my life. One of my favorite songs, John Denver's "Leaving on a Jet Plane," depicts my life travel plan. This book is like a passport stamped with my travels (life experiences), the airplane/pilot is me, the airplane hangar is my life before God, the runway is my journey through life, the boarding gate is the earth, the airplane maintenance checklist is God's plan for me, and the air traffic controller is God. When I became God's messenger, I have begun the most important travel to my final destination: heaven.

God is the author of this book, and I am in awe of how amazing He is! He has carefully planned my life to perfectly align with the chapters of this book, and He gracefully tied them all to my current situation as a traveler. The table below explains it a little bit more.

Life of a Plane	My Life as a Traveler	Chapter
An airplane is being built.	God created me.	Chapter 1: Why Me, God?
The plane sits inside a hangar until it is ready for service.	I stayed in the dark before I got saved.	Chapter 2: Staying in the Dark
Lights turned on inside hangar, the plane is ready for service, and it comes out of the hangar.	God turned on the light for me when I got saved.	Chapter 3: Let There be Light
The plane is guided by the air traffic controller and moves slowly along the runway until it reaches the boarding gate.	God guides me through my journey by listening to His voice.	Chapter 4: Hearing God's Voice
The plane remains at the boarding gate until the maintenance checklist has been completed.	I stay on earth until my work—sharing His Word—for God has been completed	Chapter 5: I Am God's Messenger

The pilot waits until the air traffic controller gives the go-ahead for takeoff.	I wait patiently for God and live in faith every day until God is ready for me to leave my earthly life.	Chapter 6: Live in Faith Everyday
The air traffic controller clears the plane for takeoff.	My work here on earth is done, and I travel for my destination.	Chapter 7: Leaving a Legacy

Are you a life traveler? Can you imagine leaving on a jet plane?

My Final Itinerary

Now that I have reached my golden years, it feels partially unreal and exciting to know that my path toward the promised land (my final destination) is getting much closer. I have a vision that the remainder of my years means passing through a tunnel and reaching the end of the tunnel means I have arrived at the promised land. I also have a vision that I need to focus on the candle that is lit at the end of the tunnel. I believe Jesus is becoming brighter and brighter as I get closer to Him. When the candle reaches its maximum brightness, it means I am holding Jesus's hands as He leads me toward the heavenly gates—the entrance to the promised land.

I imagine heaven is a place where the sun is always shining like a beautiful, warm summer morning. I imagine there are endless fields of beautiful flowers, colorful birds and butterflies flying, comfortably warm weather, and everyone has a peaceful smile. Sickness, troubles, and worries do not exist in heaven. There is only peace, joy, and love. Aren't peace, joy, and love what God wants us to have and experience while we are here on earth?

My final "itinerary" is not a direct flight. It has two "legs," meaning I have two plans to complete before I reach my final destination with God. The first plan requires my entire devotion and love for God with all my heart, soul, and mind (the First Commandment). To be honest, this devotional love was not something I was good at, and I am still working on it. I need to constantly remind myself to fully lean on and trust Him with every act, thought, and feeling. I need to focus on believing that nothing is impossible with God. I need to remember that His joy is my strength and stronghold. I need to live by God's Word and never look back. I need to be like Jesus.

The second plan is to love myself and loving others (the Second Commandment). I need to take time for myself and laugh more often. I need to enjoy traveling with my husband until we settle on a place where we can retire. I need to do more of God's work and help others. I need to focus on not deviating from my final plans until I meet Jesus at the end of my tunnel.

I pray that the analogy of my life as a traveler leaving on a jet plane brings a smile and connection with you. God comforted me with the wisdom to write this last chapter of my story. Our travel plans are different, and God arranges for it all. He is the almighty God who ensures that we do not deviate from His plan, and if we do, He redirects us to the right path.

Would you be willing to reevaluate your current travel plans and allow God to redirect your path if necessary? Can you try to be patient and not be anxious while you wait expectantly for God to change your plans? He may not arrive early, but He is never late!

Betty Lou: A Mother's Love

Do not be anxious about anything but in every situation by prayer
and petition with thanksgiving present your requests with God.
—Philippians 4:6–7 (NIV)

Betty Lou was introduced to me by one of my friends who worked with her. Betty Lou hides her shyness behind her beautiful smile. The few times we were in a group, I could tell how engaged she was by her body actions, but her preference was not to talk too much in fear of saying something wrong. The few times she did speak up, she was right on!

In a group gathering, there is always someone who tends to be shy and takes time to get used to speaking—that's Betty Lou—and there's always someone who has no problem speaking and sometimes has a hard time being quiet—and that's me. Betty Lou and I are total opposites in a group setting, but when we had our one-on-one interview, her shyness disappeared. She was very engaged, and we had the most wonderful conversation. She really opened up her feelings.

Betty Lou raised two beautiful men, and neither of them live in the same state as her. Both men are married, but one of them is getting a divorce. As a mother, we worry about our children 24/7, but Betty Lou is a supreme worrier—much more than any other mother. There were many times when her worry consumed her, especially with her son whose marriage is falling apart. Betty Lou's heart breaks for him, and the long distance adds to the heartache.

I can feel and hear her love and worry for her children in her voice. As a mother, it is a natural feeling, but it can become unhealthy.

I said, "What if your son fell backward—and a train was coming at an extremely high speed? Would you push him aside and risk your life by being hit by the train?"

She said, "Absolutely!"

That is unconditional love. Well, God has a greater unconditional love for us, and we need to completely lean on Him and trust Him.

Betty Lou is interested in learning more about the scriptures that teach us to be courageous and not be afraid.

The legacy Betty Lou wants to leave behind is her unconditional love for her children—just like God's promise of His unconditional love for her. She wants her children to remember that she was always there for them—no matter what. She also wants to be remembered as a kind and loving daughter for her mother and a true and funny friend.

I look forward to getting to know Betty Lou, and I believe our interview was the first of many intimate conversations we will have. I am excited to hear what she has to say in our next group meeting, and I feel blessed to have found a true, funny, and warmhearted friend.

Nestor: Welcome Home, Son

My father's house has many rooms; if that were not so, would I have told you that I am going there to prepare a place for you?
—John 14:2 (NIV)

Nestor was from a very loving family. Unfortunately, at a very young age, both of his parents died due to illness and left him as an orphan and responsible for his two younger brothers. Fortunately, his grandmother, aunts, uncles, and cousins lived very close and were around them to show their love. Nestor is a child of God. Even with limited financial resources and sometimes in survival mode, he never lost hope. During his struggles, he became more prayerful, he confided his problems to God through prayer, and his faith grew stronger and stronger each day.

Today, Nestor has his own family, is married to a loving wife, and has two beautiful children. He works the night shift while his family sleeps, and during the day, he spends time with his family after only a few hours of sleep. Nestor is very careful about spending his money, but he is always willing to help someone financially if needed.

I asked Nestor what message he wants to leave behind when God calls him to heaven, and his response was too beautiful not to share. He wants his family and friends to know that he may not have been the coolest, or the richest, or the most popular person, but he has one of the strongest faiths in God. "Everything is possible with God. Faith will make your heart's desire happen."

I am truly blessed to have a close relationship with Nestor. At the end of each of our communications, he never fails to say, "To God be the glory." What a beautiful and important lesson for all of us to learn from someone so young. I have a vision of God calling Nestor to heaven with a big welcoming smile on His face saying "Welcome home, son"—and Nestor's parents are standing next to God with wide-open arms to embrace him. Nestor will leave behind a legacy of strong faith and hope for all of us.

Michaela: Leaving a Legacy of Love

> Dear children, I will be with you only a little longer.
> And as I told the Jewish leaders, you will search for
> me, but you can't come where I am going.
> —John 13:33 (NLT)

Michaela is a lovely woman who does not live very far from me. Her husband knew my husband, and we were later introduced. Michaela is in her sixties, and she is a strong, healthy woman. Her physical fitness is attributable to her many years as a fitness teacher. What an inspiration for us to look so strong and healthy like her during our retirement years!

Michaela is enjoying the life of an empty nester and lives comfortably with her husband. They enjoy going out and are very fond of dining at a Chinese restaurant in the heart of our town. I know that for a fact because we often see them there. Our husbands share a passion for politics, and Michaela and I share a passion for God. In my brief interview with her, we discussed what she would want to leave behind for her children.

Michaela said, "I hope my kids learned from me and practiced and not about what I have to leave behind." Leaving behind love or the ways that someone displayed love is such a beautiful legacy. We learned that everything on earth, including our material possessions, is temporary. Our actions here on earth are what matter most.

Michaela's story is the last of the beautiful stories of my friends who graciously shared their stories with me. I am truly blessed to have all of them in my life.

God Is Our Finisher

> Let us run with endurance the race that is set before us,
> looking unto Jesus, the author and finisher of our faith.
> —Hebrews 12:1–2 (NKJV)

In chapter 1, we learned that God is our Author. In this chapter, we also learned that He has been the Author of this book. Just like we need to finish the end of this chapter and the end of this book, we also need to learn that God is our Finisher. Any plan He has for you is authored by Him and will be finished by Him, according to His will. When we finish our work here on earth, we leave behind a legacy that God planned for us.

With God's help, I am hoping to leave a legacy that will put a smile on God's face when I see Him. This book—and possibly other books—will be the legacy that I leave behind for my family, friends, and brothers and sisters in Christ. I pray that I leave a legacy of loving God and others.

Do I even matter? Yes, you do!

> God has given each of you a gift from his great
> variety of spiritual gifts. Use them well to serve one
> another. (1 Peter 4:10 NLT)

We all matter to God. No matter where you are today in your spiritual maturity—whether you are a beginner, intermediate, or advanced believer—God loves you just as you are. He has given each of us a gift. Only you can discern and discover if you open your heart for Him and hear His voice. There is no need for us to plan for anything; we just need to lean on Him, follow His lead, and trust Him. He has a plan or story for you to share—just like I was able to share my stories and the stories of others. God is our Author, Comforter, Deliverer, Counselor, Rewarder, Protector, and Finisher. He is the Alpha and the Omega. He is our almighty God who can do it all.

I pray that you have enjoyed reading this book and pray that the stories resonated with you and helped you. I give thanks to God for the wisdom and strength to write my first book. May the almighty God bless you—and peace be with you.

Notes from Chapter 7

- Have you made any travel plans lately?
- Where were you planning to go?

Appendix A

The L.I.F.E. Graph

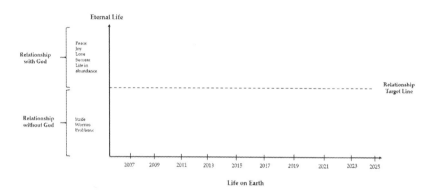

Appendix B

Be Not Afraid – 30/31 Day Challenge

Day 1: 1 Chronicles 22:13 – Then you will have success if you are careful to observe the decrees and laws that the LORD gave Moses for Israel. Be strong and courageous. _Do not be afraid or discouraged_.

Day 2: 1 Chronicles 28:20 – David also said to Solomon his son, "Be strong and courageous, and do the work. _Do not be afraid or discouraged_, for the LORD God, my God, is with you. He will not fail you or forsake you until all the work for the service of the temple of the LORD is finished

Day 3: 2 Chronicles 20:15 – He said: "Listen, King Jehoshaphat and all who live in Judah and Jerusalem! This is what the LORD says to you: _'Do not be afraid or discouraged_ because of this vast army. For the battle is not yours, but God's.

Day 4: 2 Chronicles 20:17 – You will not have to fight this battle. Take up your positions; stand firm and see the deliverance the LORD will give you, Judah and Jerusalem. _Do not be afraid; do not be discouraged_. Go out to face them tomorrow, and the LORD will be with you.'"

Day 5: 1 Corinthians 10:13 – No temptation has overtaken you except what is common to mankind. And God is faithful; he will not let you be tempted beyond what you can bear. But when you are tempted, he will also provide a way out so that you can endure it.

Day 6: 2 Corinthians 4:16 – Therefore we do not lose heart. Though outwardly we are wasting away, yet inwardly we are being renewed day by day.

Day 7: 1 John 4:18 – There is no fear in love. But perfect love dries out fear, because fear has to do with punishment. The one who fears is not made perfect in love.

Day 8: 1 Peter 5:7 – Cast all your anxiety on Him because He cares for you.

Day 9: 2 Timothy 1:7 – For the Spirit God gave us does not make us timid, but gives us power, love and self-discipline.

Day 10: Deuteronomy 31:6 – _Be strong and courageous_. Do not be afraid or terrified because of them, for the Lord your God goes with you; he will never leave you nor forsake you

Day 11: Genesis 28:15 – "I am with you and will watch over you wherever you go, and I will bring you back to this land. I will not leave you until I have done what I have promised you."

Day 12: Hebrews 13:5 – Keep your lives free from the love of money and be content with what you have, because God has said, "Never will I leave you; never will I forsake you."

Day 13: Isaiah 41:10 – So _do not fear_, for I am with you; do not be dismayed, for I am your God. I will strengthen you and help you; I will uphold you with my righteous right hand.

Day 14: Isaiah 44:2 – This is what the LORD says-- he who made you, who formed you in the womb, and who will help you: _Do not be afraid_, Jacob, my servant, Jeshurun, whom I have chosen.

Day 15: Jeremiah 20:11 – But the LORD is with me like a mighty warrior; so my persecutors will stumble and not prevail. They will fail and be thoroughly disgraced; their dishonor will never be forgotten.

Day 16: Joshua 1:9 – Have I not commanded you? Be strong and courageous. _Do not be afraid; do not be discouraged_, for the LORD your God will be with you wherever you go."

Day 17: Luke 1:37 – For no word from God will ever fail

Day 18: Luke 10:19 – I have given you authority to trample on snakes and scorpions and to overcome all the power of the enemy; nothing will harm you.

Day 19: Mark 5:36 – Overhearing what they said, Jesus told him, "_Don't be afraid_; just believe."

Day 20: Matthew 6:34 – Therefore do not worry about tomorrow, for tomorrow will worry about itself. Each day has enough trouble of its own.

Day 21: Matthew 11:28 – Come to me all you who are heavy and burdened and I will give you rest.

Day 22: Matthew 19:26 – Jesus looked at them and said, "With man this is impossible, but with God all things are possible."

Day 23: Nahum 1:7 – The Lord is good, a strength and stronghold in the day of trouble. He knows those who take refuge and trust in Him.

Day 24: Numbers 14:9 – Only do not rebel against the LORD. And do not be afraid of the people of the land, because we will devour them. Their protection is gone, but the LORD is with us. _Do not be afraid_ of them."

Day 25: Philippians 4:6 – Do not be anxious about anything, but in every situation, by prayer and petition, with thanksgiving, present your requests to God.

Day 26: Psalm 27:1 – Of David. The LORD is my light and my salvation-- whom shall I fear? The LORD is the stronghold of my life-- of whom shall I be afraid?

Day 27: Psalm 27:14 – Wait for the LORD; be strong and take heart and wait for the LORD.

Day 28: Psalm 56:3-4 –When I am afraid, I will put my trust in You. In God, whose word I praise, In God I have put my trust; I shall _not be afraid_. What can _mere_ man do to me?

Day 29: Psalm 91:5 – You will _not fear_ the terror of night, nor the arrow that flies by day

Day 30: Revelations 21:4 – He will wipe every tear from their eyes. There will be no more death' or mourning or crying or pain, for the old order of things has passed away."

Appendix C

Book of Proverbs

(Sofia's simplified version)

1. Be Prudent – to be balanced and conduct yourself wisely
2. Seek understanding of God's Word and will of others. Be compassionate.
3. Live by faith lean on and trust Him with all your heart, mind and not your own understanding
4. Get skillful and godly wisdom
5. Do not hate or dread anything but sin
6. Seven things that the Lord hates: proud look, lying, murder, wicked heart, feet swift to evil, sow discord and abomination
7. Keep my commandments and live. Keep my law and teaching as the apple of your eye
8. Speak words that are righteous and true
9. Reverential and worshipful fear of the Lord – this is the beginning of wisdom.
10. Walk with integrity, be honest and trustworthy
11. He who diligently seeks God, seeks favor.
12. Anxiety weighs a man's heart down, encouraging word makes it glad.
13. Every prudent man deals with knowledge, but a fool flaunts his folly.

14. Don't hold bitterness in your heart
15. Power of words – use your mouth to heal, restore and uplift
16. Pride and arrogance are extremely offensive to the Lord. Do not gossip.
17. Develop a happy heart
18. Death and life are in the power of the tongue
19. The reverent, worshipful fear of the Lord seeks to life and he who has it rests satisfied
20. Wait for the Lord and He will rescue you
21. He who guards his mouth and his tongue keeps himself from troubles
22. The reward of humility is riches and honor and life
23. As he thinks in his heart so is he
24. For a righteous man falls <u>seven</u> times and rises again
25. If your enemy is hungry, give him food to eat; if he is thirsty, give him water to drink.
26. Whoever digs a pit shall fall into himself and he who rolls a stone it will return upon him
27. Let another man praise you and not on your lips; a stranger and not on your mouth
28. The righteous are bold as a lion. Be as bold as a lion in your faith.
29. Have a vision. Believe!
30. Don't be foolish in exalting yourself
31. Be a Virtuous Woman.

Appendix D

Topical Index

(NIV unless otherwise stated)

Anxiety
Proverbs 12:25 – Anxiety weighs down the heart, but a kind word cheers it up.

Beatitude
Matthew 5:3-12
Blessed are the poor in spirit, for theirs is the kingdom of heaven
Blessed are those who mourn, for they shall be comforted
Blessed are the meek, for they shall inherit the earth
Blessed are those who hunger and thirst for righteousness sake for they shall be completely satisfied
Blessed are the merciful, for they shall obtain mercy
Blessed are the pure in heart, for they shall see God
Blessed are the peacemakers, for they shall be called sons of God
Blessed are those who are persecuted for righteousness sake, for theirs is the kingdom of heaven
Blessed are you when people revile and persecute you and say all kind of evil things on account of me
Be glad and supremely joyful for your reward in heaven is great

Become like Christ

2 Corinthians 3:18 – And we all, who with unveiled faces contemplate the Lord's glory, are being transformed into his image with ever-increasing glory, which comes from the Lord, who is the Spirit.

2 Corinthians 5:17 – Therefore, if anyone is in Christ, the new creation has come: The old has gone, the new is here!

2 Peter 1:5-8 –Now for this very reason also, applying all diligence, in your faith supply moral excellence, and in *your* moral excellence, knowledge, and in *your* knowledge, self-control, and in *your* self-control, perseverance, and in *your* perseverance, godliness, and in *your* godliness, brotherly kindness, and in *your* brotherly kindness, love. For if these *qualities* are yours and are increasing, they render you neither useless nor unfruitful in the true knowledge of our Lord Jesus Christ

Ephesians 5:1 ESV – Therefore be imitators of God, as beloved children

Mathew 4:19 "Come, follow me," Jesus said

Matthew 10:38 – Whoever does not take up their cross and follow me is not worthy of me.

Believe

2 Chronicles 20:20b ESV - Believe in the LORD your God, and you will be established; believe his prophets, and you will succeed."

2 Corinthians 4:18 – So we fix our eyes not on what is seen, but on what is unseen, since what is seen is temporary, but what is unseen is eternal.

2 Corinthians 5:7 – For we live by faith, not by sight.

John 3:16 – For God so loved the world that he gave his one and only Son, that whoever believes in him shall not perish but have eternal life.

John 11:40 – Then Jesus said, "Did I not tell you that if you believe, you will see the glory of God?"

Luke 11:9 – "So I say to you: Ask and it will be given to you; seek and you will find; knock and the door will be opened to you.

Mark 9:23 – "'If you can'?" said Jesus. "Everything is possible for one who believes."

Matthew 21:22 – If you believe, you will receive whatever you ask for in prayer."

Blessing
John 13:17 – Now that you know these things, you will be blessed if you do them.

Born Again
1 Peter 1:3 – Praise be to the God and Father of our Lord Jesus Christ! In his great mercy he has given us new birth into a living hope through the resurrection of Jesus Christ from the dead.

Colossians 3:10 – And have put on the new self, which is being renewed in knowledge in the image of its Creator.

John 3:3 – Jesus replied, "Very truly I tell you, no one can see the kingdom of God unless they are born again."

Christ's Ambassador
2 Corinthians 5:20 – We are therefore Christ's ambassadors, as though God were making his appeal through us. We implore you on Christ's behalf: Be reconciled to God.

The Great Commission
Matthew 28:19 – Therefore go and make disciples of all nations, baptizing them in the name of the Father and of the Son and of the Holy Spirit.

Compassion
Galatians 6:2 – Carry each other's burdens, and in this way, you will fulfill the law of Christ.

Comforter (God is)
2 Corinthians 1:3-5 – Praise be to the God and Father of our Lord Jesus Christ, the Father of compassion and the God of all comfort, who comforts us in all our troubles.

Commit
Proverbs 16:3 – Commit to the LORD whatever you do, and he will establish your plans.

Comparing ourselves
Galatians 5:26 – Let us not become conceited, provoking, and envying each other.

Complaining
Philippians 2:14 – Do everything without grumbling or arguing

Deliverer (God is)
2 Samuel 22:2-3 – He said: "The LORD is my rock, my fortress and my deliverer; my God is my rock, in whom I take refuge, my shield and the horn of my salvation. He is my stronghold, my refuge and my savior-- from violent people you save me.

Exodus 14:14 – The LORD will fight for you; you need only to be still.

Counselor (God is)
John 14:26 – But the Advocate, the Holy Spirit, whom the Father will send in my name, will teach you all things and will remind you of everything I have said to you.

Divorce
Mark 10:9 – Therefore what God has joined together, let no one separate.

Dreams
Numbers 12:6 - he said, Listen to my words: "When there is a prophet among you, I, the Lord, reveal myself to them in visions, I speak to them in dreams."

Encourage
1 Thessalonians 5:11 NLT – So encourage each to other and build each other up just as you are already doing

Enemy/Evil
1 Peter 5:8 – Be alert and of sober mind. Your enemy the devil prowls around like a roaring lion looking for someone to devour.

1 Timothy 6:10 – For the love of money is a root of all kinds of evil. Some people, eager for money, have wandered from the faith and pierced themselves with many griefs.

Ephesians 4:26-28 – "In your anger do not sin": Do not let the sun go down while you are still angry, and do not give the devil a foothold. Anyone who has been stealing must steal no longer, but must work, doing something useful with their own hands, that they may have something to share with those in need.

John 10:10 – The thief comes only to steal and kill and destroy; I have come that they may have life, and have it to the full.

Luke 4:8 – Jesus answered, "It is written: 'Worship the Lord your God and serve him only.'"

Matthew 5:44 – But I tell you, love your enemies and pray for those who persecute you,.

Matthew 16:23 – Jesus turned and said to Peter, "Get behind me, Satan! You are a stumbling block to me; you do not have in mind the concerns of God, but merely human concerns."

Envy
1 Corinthians 13:6-8 – Love does not delight in evil but rejoices with the truth. It always protects, always trusts, always hopes, always perseveres. Love never fails. But where there are prophecies, they will cease; where there are tongues, they will be stilled; where there is knowledge, it will pass away.

Eternal Life
Hebrews 13:14 NLT – For this world is not our permanent home; we are looking forward to a home yet to come.

Excellence
Philippians 4:8 – Finally, brothers and sisters, whatever is true, whatever is noble, whatever is right, whatever is pure, whatever is lovely, whatever is admirable--if anything is excellent or praiseworthy--think about such things.

Faithfulness
1 Thessalonians 5:16-18 – Rejoice always, pray continually, give thanks in all circumstances; for this is God's will for you in Christ Jesus.

1 Timothy 6:12 AMP – Fight the good fight of faith

Colossians 1:4 – because we have heard of your faith in Christ Jesus and of the love you have for all God's people.

Habakkuk 2:4 – "See, the enemy is puffed up; his desires are not upright-- but the righteous person will live by his faithfulness.

Hebrews 11:1 – Now faith is confidence in what we hope for and assurance about what we do not see.

Hebrews 10:36 – You need to persevere so that when you have done the will of God, you will receive what he has promised.

Isaiah 9:1a NLT – Nevertheless, that time of darkness and despair will not go on forever.

Luke 16:10 NLT – "If you are faithful in little things, you will be faithful in large ones. But if you are dishonest in little things, you won't be honest with greater responsibilities.

Proverbs 3:5-6 – Trust in the LORD with all your heart and lean not on your own understanding; in all your ways submit to him, and he will make your paths straight.

Revelations 14:12 – This calls for patient endurance on the part of the people of God who keep his commands and remain faithful to Jesus.

Romans 10:9 ESV - Because, if you confess with your mouth that Jesus is Lord and believe in your heart that God raised him from the dead, you will be saved".

Ruth 1:16 – But Ruth replied, "Don't urge me to leave you or to turn back from you. Where you go I will go, and where you stay I will stay. Your people will be my people and your God my God.

Forgiveness

Hebrews 12:15 – See to it that no one falls short of the grace of God and that no bitter root grows up to cause trouble and defile many.

Mark 11:26 – "But if you do not forgive, neither will your Father who is in heaven forgive your transgressions."

Matthew 5:39 NIV – But I say to you, do not resist an evil person. If anyone slaps you on your right cheek, turn the other cheek also.

Matthew 6:15 – But if you do not forgive others their sins, your Father will not forgive your sins.

Matthew 18:22 – Jesus answered, "I tell you, not seven times, but seventy-seven times.

Proverbs 14:10 – Each heart knows its own bitterness, and no one else can share its joy.

Foul Language/Gossip

Ephesians 4:29 – Do not let any unwholesome talk come out of your mouths, but only what is helpful for building others up according to their needs, that it may benefit those who listen.

Leviticus 19:16, 18 – "'Do not go about spreading slander among your people. "'Do not do anything that endangers your neighbor's life. I am the LORD. "'Do not seek revenge or bear a grudge against anyone among your people, but love your neighbor as yourself. I am the LORD.

Proverbs 16:28 – A perverse person stirs up conflict, and a gossip separates close friends.

Friendship with God
Psalm 25:14 – The LORD confides in those who fear him; he makes his covenant known to them.

Frustration
Daniel 3:17 - If we are thrown into the blazing furnace, the God we serve is able to deliver us from it, and he will deliver us from Your Majesty's hand.

Giving
Acts 20:35 – In everything I did, I showed you that by this kind of hard work we must help the weak, remembering the words the Lord Jesus himself said: 'It is more blessed to give than to receive.'"

Glorify God
1 Corinthians 10:31 – So whether you eat or drink or whatever you do, do it all for the glory of God.

2 Corinthians 12:5 – I will boast about a man like that, but I will not boast about myself, except about my weaknesses.

2 Peter 1:3 – His divine power has given us everything we need for a godly life through our knowledge of him who called us by his own glory and goodness.

Matthew 5:16 – In the same way, let your light shine before others, that they may see your good deeds and glorify your Father in heaven.

Romans 11:36 – For from him and through him and for him are all things. To him be the glory forever! Amen.

Golden Rule
Luke 6:31 – Do to others as you would have them do to you.

God

2 Chronicles 30:9 – If you return to the LORD, then your fellow Israelites and your children will be shown compassion by their captors and will return to this land, for the LORD your God is gracious and compassionate. He will not turn his face from you if you return to him."

Colossians 1:16 – For in him all things were created: things in heaven and on earth, visible and invisible, whether thrones or powers or rulers or authorities; all things have been created through him and for him.

Daniel 2:21- He changes times and seasons; he deposes kings and raises up others. He gives wisdom to the wise and knowledge to the discerning.

Exodus 34:14 – Do not worship any other god, for the LORD, whose name is Jealous, is a jealous God.

Hebrews 4:12 – For the word of God is alive and active. Sharper than any double-edged sword, it penetrates even to dividing soul and spirit, joints and marrow; it judges the thoughts and attitudes of the heart.

Isaiah 44:2 CEV – I am your Creator, you were in my care, even before you were born

John 1:1 – In the beginning was the Word, and the Word was with God, and the Word was God.

John 14:6 – Jesus answered, "I am the way and the truth and the life. No one comes to the Father except through me.

John 15:5 – "I am the vine; you are the branches. If you remain in me and I in you, you will bear much fruit; apart from me you can do nothing.

Leviticus 25:17 – Do not take advantage of each other, but fear your God. I am the LORD your God.

Malachi 3:6 – "I the LORD do not change. So you, the descendants of Jacob, are not destroyed.

Revelation 1:8 "I am the Alpha and the Omega," says the Lord God, "who is, and who was, and who is to come, the Almighty."

Zephaniah 3:17 – The LORD your God is with you, the Mighty Warrior who saves. He will take great delight in you; in his love he will no longer rebuke you, but will rejoice over you with singing."

God's Children
Genesis 1:27 – So God created mankind in his own image, in the image of God he created them; male and female he created them.

God's Faithfulness/Promises/Plans
1 John 1:9 – If we confess our sins, he is faithful and just and will forgive us our sins and purify us from all unrighteousness.

Deuteronomy 1:11 – May the LORD, the God of your ancestors, increase you a thousand times and bless you as he has promised!

Deuteronomy 8:3 – e humbled you, causing you to hunger and then feeding you with manna, which neither you nor your ancestors had known, to teach you that man does not live on bread alone but on every word that comes from the mouth of the LORD.

Jeremiah 29:11 AMP – For I know the thoughts and plans that I have for you, says the Lord.

Psalm 33:1 – Sing joyfully to the LORD, you righteous; it is fitting for the upright to praise him.

God's Grace

1 Corinthians 15:10 – But by the grace of God I am what I am, and his grace to me was not without effect. No, I worked harder than all of them--yet not I, but the grace of God that was with me.

Deuteronomy 28:1 – If you fully obey the LORD your God and carefully follow all his commands I give you today, the LORD your God will set you high above all the nations on earth.

Deuteronomy 30:20 – And that you may love the LORD your God, listen to his voice, and hold fast to him. For the LORD is your life, and he will give you many years in the land he swore to give to your fathers, Abraham, Isaac and Jacob.

Ephesians 2:8-9 – For it is by grace you have been saved, through faith--and this is not from yourselves, it is the gift of God, not by works, so that no one can boast.

Ephesians 3:20 NLT – Now all glory to God, who is able, through his mighty power at work within us, to accomplish infinitely more than we might ask or think.

Psalm 67:3 – May the peoples praise you, God; may all the peoples praise you.

God's Love

Romans 8:37 – No, in all these things we are more than conquerors through him who loved us.

God's Mercy

Psalm 57:1b – Have mercy on me, my God, have mercy on me, for in you I take refuge. I will take refuge in the shadow of your wings until the disaster has passed.

God's Presence

Matthew 18:20 – For where two or three gather in my name, there am I with them."

God's Perfect Timing

Habakkuk 2:4 – "See, the enemy is puffed up; his desires are not upright-- but the righteous person will live by his faithfulness.

God's Voice

1 Kings 19:12 – After the earthquake came a fire, but the LORD was not in the fire. And after the fire came a gentle whisper.

Hebrews 3:15 – As has just been said: "Today, if you hear his voice, do not harden your hearts as you did in the rebellion."

God's Word

2 Timothy 3:17 – so that the servant of God may be thoroughly equipped for every good work.

Luke 4:4 – Jesus answered, "It is written: 'Man shall not live on bread alone.'"

Mark 8:35 – For whoever wants to save their life will lose it, but whoever loses their life for me and for the gospel will save it.

Matthew 4:4 – Jesus answered, "It is written: 'Man shall not live on bread alone, but on every word that comes from the mouth of God.'"

Proverbs 2:2 – turning your ear to wisdom and applying your heart to understanding.

Proverbs 8:8 – All the words of my mouth are just; none of them is crooked or perverse.

Psalm 119:97 – Oh, how I love your law! I meditate on it all day long.

Psalm 119:105 NIV – Your Word is a lamp to my feet and a light to my path

Godliness
1 Timothy 6:11 – But you, man of God, flee from all this, and pursue righteousness, godliness, faith, love, endurance and gentleness.

Goodness
1 Timothy 4:7 – Have nothing to do with godless myths and old wives' tales; rather, train yourself to be godly.

Proverbs 11:27 – Whoever seeks good finds favor, but evil comes to one who searches for it.

Romans 12:21 – Do not be overcome by evil, but overcome evil with good.

Happiness
James 1:25 – But whoever looks intently into the perfect law that gives freedom, and continues in it--not forgetting what they have heard, but doing it--they will be blessed in what they do.

Healing
Exodus 15:26 – He said, "If you listen carefully to the LORD your God and do what is right in his eyes, if you pay attention to his commands and keep all his decrees, I will not bring on you any of the diseases I brought on the Egyptians, for I am the LORD, who heals you."

Matthew 4:24 – News about him spread all over Syria, and people brought to him all who were ill with various diseases, those suffering severe pain, the demon-possessed, those having seizures, and the paralyzed; and he healed them.

Philippians 3:12-13 – Not that I have already obtained all this, or have already arrived at my goal, but I press on to take hold of that for which Christ Jesus took hold of me. Brothers and sisters, I do not consider myself yet to have taken hold of it. But one thing I do: Forgetting what is behind and straining toward what is ahead,

Heart
2 Chronicles 16:9 – For the eyes of the LORD range throughout the earth to strengthen those whose hearts are fully committed to him. You have done a foolish thing, and from now on you will be at war."

1 Kings 8:61 – And may your hearts be fully committed to the LORD our God, to live by his decrees and obey his commands, as at this time."

1 Samuel 16:7b – The LORD does not look at the things people look at. People look at the outward appearance, but the LORD looks at the heart."

Ezekiel 3:10 – And he said to me, "Son of man, listen carefully and take to heart all the words I speak to you.

Ezekiel 11:19 – I will give them an undivided heart and put a new spirit in them; I will remove from them their heart of stone and give them a heart of flesh.

Galatians 6:9 – Let us not become weary in doing good, for at the proper time we will reap a harvest if we do not give up.

Hebrews 3:7-8 – So, as the Holy Spirit says: "Today, if you hear his voice, do not harden your hearts as you did in the rebellion, during the time of testing in the wilderness,

John 14:1 – "Do not let your hearts be troubled. You believe in God; believe also in me.

Lamentations 3:40-41 – Let us examine our ways and test them, and let us return to the LORD. Let us lift up our hearts and our hands to God in heaven.

Matthew 12:34 – You brood of vipers, how can you who are evil say anything good? For the mouth speaks what the heart is full of.

Matthew 15:18 – But the things that come out of a person's mouth come from the heart, and these defile them.

Proverbs 5:12 – You will say, "How I hated discipline! How my heart spurned correction!

Proverbs 15:13 – A happy heart makes the face cheerful, but heartache crushes the spirit.

Proverbs 17:22 – A cheerful heart is good medicine, but a crushed spirit dries up the bones.

Proverbs 23:7 NKJV – For as he thinks in his heart, so *is* he

Proverbs 27:19 – As water reflects the face, so one's life reflects the heart.

Psalm 51:10 – Create in me a pure heart, O God, and renew a steadfast spirit within me.

Psalm 119:11 – I have hidden your word in my heart that I might not sin against you.

Holy Spirit
Galatians 5:16-17 – So I say, walk by the Spirit, and you will not gratify the desires of the flesh. For the flesh desires what is contrary to the Spirit, and the Spirit what is contrary to the flesh. They are in conflict with each other, so that you are not to do whatever you want.

Galatians 5:22-23 – But the fruit of the Spirit is love, joy, peace, forbearance, kindness, goodness, faithfulness, gentleness and self-control. Against such things there is no law

Jude 1:20-21 – But you, dear friends, by building yourselves up in your most holy faith and praying in the Holy Spirit, keep yourselves in God's love as you wait for the mercy of our Lord Jesus Christ to bring you to eternal life.

Romans 8:14 – For those who are led by the Spirit of God are the children of God.

Honesty
Ephesians 4:15 – Instead, speaking the truth in love, we will grow to become in every respect the mature body of him who is the head, that is, Christ.

Hope
Proverbs 13:12 – Hope deferred makes the heart sick, but a longing fulfilled is a tree of life.

Romans 15:13 – May the God of hope fill you with all joy and peace as you trust in him, so that you may overflow with hope by the power of the Holy Spirit

Zechariah 9:12 – Return to your fortress, you prisoners of hope; even now I announce that I will restore twice as much to you.

Humility

2 Corinthians 10:18 – For it is not the one who commends himself who is approved, but the one whom the Lord commends.

1 Peter 5:6 NKJV – Therefore humble yourselves under the mighty hand of God, that He may exalt you in due time.

Galatians 6:4 – Each one should test their own actions. Then they can take pride in themselves alone, without comparing themselves to someone else.

James 1:21 – Therefore, get rid of all moral filth and the evil that is so prevalent and humbly accept the word planted in you, which can save you.

James 4:6 – But he gives us more grace. That is why Scripture says: "God opposes the proud but shows favor to the humble."

Matthew 18:4 – Therefore, whoever takes the lowly position of this child is the greatest in the kingdom of heaven.

Micah 6:8 – He has shown you, O mortal, what is good. And what does the LORD require of you? To act justly and to love mercy and to walk humbly with your God.

Obadiah 3 – The pride of your heart has deceived you, you who live in the clefts of the rocks and make your home on the heights, you who say to yourself, 'Who can bring me down to the ground?'

Philippians 2:3 – Do nothing out of selfish ambition or vain conceit. Rather, in humility value others above yourselves.

Proverbs 29:23 – Pride brings a person low, but the lowly in spirit gain honor.

Proverbs 30:32 – "If you play the fool and exalt yourself, or if you plan evil, clap your hand over your mouth!

Integrity

Proverbs 10:9 – Whoever walks in integrity walks securely, but whoever takes crooked paths will be found out.

Psalm 25:21 – May integrity and uprightness protect me, because my hope, LORD, is in you.

Joy

Ecclesiastes 5:18 – This is what I have observed to be good: that it is appropriate for a person to eat, to drink and to find satisfaction in their toilsome labor under the sun during the few days of life God has given them--for this is their lot.

Judging

Luke 6:36-38 – Be merciful, just as your Father is merciful. "Do not judge, and you will not be judged. Do not condemn, and you will not be condemned. Forgive, and you will be forgiven. Give, and it will be given to you. A good measure, pressed down, shaken together and running over, will be poured into your lap. For with the measure you use, it will be measured to you."

Matthew 7:1 – "Do not judge, or you too will be judged."

Romans 14:10 – You, then, why do you judge your brother or sister? Or why do you treat them with contempt? For we will all stand before God's judgment seat.

Romans 14:12 NIV – So then, each of us will give an account of ourselves to God.

Kindness
1 Thessalonians 5:15-17 AMP – See that no one repays another with evil for evil, but always seek that which is <u>good</u> for one another and for all people

Listening
Luke 8:18 – Therefore consider carefully how you listen. Whoever has will be given more; whoever does not have, even what they think they have will be taken from them."

Love
1 Corinthians 13:4-8 - Love is patient, love is kind. It does not envy, it does not boast, it is not proud. It does not dishonor others, it is not self-seeking, it is not easily angered, it keeps no record of wrongs. Love does not delight in evil but rejoices with the truth. t always protects, always trusts, always hopes, always perseveres. Love never fails.

1 Corinthians 13:13 - And now these three remain: faith, hope and love. But the greatest of these is love.

1 John 4:18 – There is no fear in love. But perfect love drives out fear, because fear has to do with punishment. The one who fears is not made perfect in love.

Love Others
1 Corinthians 10:24 – No one should seek their own good, but the good of others.

1 John 1:7 NLT – But if we are living in the light, as God is in the light, then we have fellowship with each other."

Colossians 3:12 – Therefore, as God's chosen people, holy and dearly loved, clothe yourselves with compassion, kindness, humility, gentleness and patience.

Ephesians 5:16 – making the most of every opportunity, because the days are evil.

Galatians 6:2 – Carry each other's burdens, and in this way you will fulfill the law of Christ.

John 13:35 – By this everyone will know that you are my disciples, if you love one another."

Luke 6:35 – But love your enemies, do good to them, and lend to them without expecting to get anything back. Then your reward will be great, and you will be children of the Most High, because he is kind to the ungrateful and wicked.

Proverbs 3:28 – Do not say to your neighbor, "Come back tomorrow and I'll give it to you"-- when you already have it with you

Proverbs 11:25 – A generous person will prosper; whoever refreshes others will be refreshed.

Proverbs 24:17 – Do not gloat when your enemy falls; when they stumble, do not let your heart rejoice,

Proverbs 25:21-22 – If your enemy is hungry, give him food to eat; if he is thirsty, give him water to drink. In doing this, you will heap burning coals on his head, and the LORD will reward you.

Loving God
Deuteronomy 6:5 – Love the LORD your God with all your heart and with all your soul and with all your strength.

Matthew 22:37 ESV - You shall love the Lord your God with all your heart and with all your soul and with all your mind. That is the great and first commandment.

Romans 8:28 NKJV – And we know that all things work together for good to those who love God, to those who are the called according to His purpose

No Record of Wrongs
Romans 4:8 – Blessed is the one whose sin the Lord will never count against them.

Obedience
1 John 2:6 – Whoever claims to live in him must live as Jesus did.

1 John 2:17 – The world and its desires pass away, but whoever does the will of God lives forever.

Colossians 1:10 ESV – So as to walk in the manner worthy of the Lord, fully pleasing to Him: bearing good fruit in every good work and increasing in the knowledge of God being strengthened with all power, according to His glorious might, for all endurance and patience with joy.

Deuteronomy 13:4 – It is the LORD your God you must follow, and him you must revere. Keep his commands and obey him; serve him and hold fast to him.

John 8:12 ESV – Again, Jesus spoke to them, saying, 'I am the light of the world. Whoever follows me wall not walk in darkness, but will have the light of life."

John 8:31-32 – To the Jews who had believed him, Jesus said, "If you hold to my teaching, you are really my disciples. Then you will know the truth, and the truth will set you free."

Psalm 37:23 – The LORD makes firm the steps of the one who delights in him

Patience
1 Peter 2:20 – But how is it to your credit if you receive a beating for doing wrong and endure it? But if you suffer for doing good and you endure it, this is commendable before God

Isaiah 40:31 – but those who hope in the LORD will renew their strength. They will soar on wings like eagles; they will run and not grow weary, they will walk and not be faint.

James 1:12 – Blessed is the one who perseveres under trial because, having stood the test, that person will receive the crown of life that the Lord has promised to those who love him.

James 1:19 - 20 – My dear brothers and sisters, take note of this: Everyone should be quick to listen, slow to speak and slow to become angry, because human anger does not produce the righteousness that God desires.

Luke 21:19 – Stand firm, and you will win life

Proverbs 20:22 – Do not say, "I'll pay you back for this wrong!" Wait for the LORD, and he will avenge you.

Psalm 37:7 – Be still before the LORD and wait patiently for him; do not fret when people succeed in their ways, when they carry out their wicked schemes

Peace

1 Peter 3:11 – They must turn from evil and do good; they must seek peace and pursue it.

1 Thessalonians 4:11 – and to make it your ambition to lead a quiet life: You should mind your own business and work with your hands, just as we told you

1 Timothy 6:6 – But godliness with contentment is great gain.

Isaiah 26:3 – You will keep in perfect peace those whose minds are steadfast, because they trust in you.

John 14:27 – Peace I leave with you; my peace I give you. I do not give to you as the world gives. Do not let your hearts be troubled and do not be afraid.

Luke 10:5 – "When you enter a house, first say, 'Peace to this house.'

Numbers 6:26 – The LORD turn his face toward you and give you peace.

Pleasing God

1 Thessalonians 2:4 – On the contrary, we speak as those approved by God to be entrusted with the gospel. We are not trying to please people but God, who tests our hearts.

Praising God

1 Chronicles 16:28 – Ascribe to the LORD, all you families of nations, ascribe to the LORD glory and strength.

Philippians 4:8 – Finally, brothers and sisters, whatever is true, whatever is noble, whatever is right, whatever is pure, whatever is lovely, whatever is admirable--if anything is excellent or praiseworthy--think about such things.

Power of Words

2 Timothy 2:16 – Avoid godless chatter, because those who indulge in it will become more and more ungodly.

Luke 6:45 – A good man brings good things out of the good stored up in his heart, and an evil man brings evil things out of the evil stored up in his heart. For the mouth speaks what the heart is full of.

Proverbs 4:4 – Then he taught me, and he said to me, "Take hold of my words with all your heart; keep my commands, and you will live.

Proverbs 8:8 – All the words of my mouth are just; none of them is crooked or perverse.

Proverbs 15:1 – A gentle answer turns away wrath, but a harsh word stirs up anger.

Proverbs 16:32 – Better a patient person than a warrior, one with self-control than one who takes a city.

Proverbs 18:21 – The tongue has the power of life and death, and those who love it will eat its fruit.

Proverbs 21:23 – Those who guard their mouths and their tongues keep themselves from calamity.

Proverbs 23:7a NASB – For as he thinks within himself, so he is.

Psalm 141:3 – Set a guard over my mouth, LORD; keep watch over the door of my lips.

Prayer

Lamentations 3:22-26 AMP – It is because of the Lord's mercy and loving kindness that we are not consumed because His compassion never fails. They are new every morning; great and abundant is Your stability and faithfulness. The Lord is my portion and my inheritance therefore I have hope in Him and wait expectantly for Him."

Micah 7:7-8 – But as for me, I watch in hope for the LORD, I wait for God my Savior; my God will hear me. Do not gloat over me, my enemy! Though I have fallen, I will rise. Though I sit in darkness, the LORD will be my light.

Psalm 23

> The LORD is my shepherd; I shall not want.
> He makes me lie down in green pastures;
> He leads me beside quiet waters.
> He restores my soul;
> He guides me in the paths of righteousness for the sake of His name.
> Even though I walk through the valley of the shadow of death, I will fear no evil,
> For You are with me;
> Your rod and Your staff, they comfort me.
> You prepare a table before me in the presence of my enemies.
> You anoint my head with oil; my cup overflows.
> Surely goodness and mercy will follow me all the days of my life,
> and I will dwell in the house of the LORD forever.

Pride
1 John 2:15 – Do not love the world or anything in the world. If anyone loves the world, love for the Father is not in them.

Protector (God is)
Psalm 18:2 – Do not love the world or anything in the world. If anyone loves the world, love for the Father is not in them.

Prudence
Proverbs 1:4 – for giving prudence to those who are simple, knowledge and discretion to the young

Redeemer
Psalm 19:14 – Let the words of my mouth and the meditation of my heart be acceptable to your sight, O Lord. My rock and my redeemer.

Renewal of Mind
Colossians 3:3 – For you died, and your life is now hidden with Christ in God.

Ephesians 4:22-24 – You were taught, with regard to your former way of life, to put off your old self, which is being corrupted by its deceitful desires; to be made new in the attitude of your minds; and to put on the new self, created to be like God in true righteousness and holiness.

Romans 12:2 AMP – And do not be conformed to this world but be transformed by the renewal of your mind so that you may prove what the will of God is, that which is <u>good</u> and acceptable and perfect.

Reward
2 Corinthians 9:6 – Remember this: Whoever sows sparingly will also reap sparingly, and whoever sows generously will also reap generously.

Galatians 6:7 AMP - For whatever a man sows, this and only this he will reap

Hebrews 11:6 AMP – But without faith, it is impossible to please Him, for whoever comes near to God must believe that God exists and that He rewards those seek Him."

Mark 4:24 – "Consider carefully what you hear," he continued. "With the measure you use, it will be measured to you--and even more.

Respect
Titus 2:7 – In everything set them an example by doing what is good. In your teaching show integrity, seriousness.

Reverential Fear of God
Proverbs 15:33 – Wisdom's instruction is to fear the LORD, and humility comes before honor.

Proverbs 19:23 – The fear of the LORD leads to life; then one rests content, untouched by trouble.

Proverbs 22:4 – Humility is the fear of the LORD; its wages are riches and honor and life.

Righteousness
James 4:17 – If anyone, then, knows the good they ought to do and doesn't do it, it is sin for them.

Proverbs 28:1 - The wicked flee though no one pursues, but the righteous are as bold as a lion.

Seasons
Ecclesiastes 3:1 – everything on earth has its own time and its own season

Self-control
Proverbs 25:28 – Like a city whose walls are broken through is a person who lacks self-control.

Selection
Matthew 20:16 – "So the last will be first, and the first will be last."

Seeking God

1 Chronicles 22:19 –Now devote your heart and soul to seeking the LORD your God. Begin to build the sanctuary of the LORD God, so that you may bring the ark of the covenant of the LORD and the sacred articles belonging to God into the temple that will be built for the Name of the LORD."

1 Chronicles 28:9 – "And you, my son Solomon, acknowledge the God of your father, and serve him with wholehearted devotion and with a willing mind, for the LORD searches every heart and understands every desire and every thought. If you seek him, he will be found by you; but if you forsake him, he will reject you forever.

Hosea 5:15 – Then I will return to my lair until they have borne their guilt and seek my face-- in their misery they will earnestly seek me."

Hosea 6:1 – "Come, let us return to the LORD. He has torn us to pieces but he will heal us; he has injured us but he will bind up our wounds.

Hosea 10:12 – Sow righteousness for yourselves, reap the fruit of unfailing love, and break up your unplowed ground; for it is time to seek the LORD, until he comes and showers his righteousness on you.

Hosea 12:6 – But you must return to your God; maintain love and justice, and wait for your God always.

Jeremiah 29:13 NIV - You will seek me and find me when you seek me with all your heart

Job 5:8 – "But if I were you, I would appeal to God; I would lay my cause before him.

Job 22:21 – "Submit to God and be at peace with him; in this way prosperity will come to you.

Matthew 6:33 – But seek first his kingdom and his righteousness, and all these things will be given to you as well.

Psalm 27:4 – One thing I ask from the LORD, this only do I seek: that I may dwell in the house of the LORD all the days of my life, to gaze on the beauty of the LORD and to seek him in his temple.

Psalm 63:1 – A psalm of David. When he was in the Desert of Judah. You, God, are my God, earnestly I seek you; I thirst for you, my whole being longs for you, in a dry and parched land where there is no water.

Servant's Heart
1 Corinthians 4:2 – Now it is required that those who have been given a trust must prove faithful.

1 Peter 4:10 – Each of you should use whatever gift you have received to serve others, as faithful stewards of God's grace in its various forms.

1 Peter 5:5 – In the same way, you who are younger, submit yourselves to your elders. All of you, clothe yourselves with humility toward one another, because, "God opposes the proud but shows favor to the humble."

2 Timothy 2:24 – And the Lord's servant must not be quarrelsome but must be kind to everyone, able to teach, not resentful.

Colossians 3:23 NASB – Whatever you do, do your work heartily, as for the Lord rather than for men.

Ephesians 4:1-3 – As a prisoner for the Lord, then, I urge you to live a life worthy of the calling you have received. Be completely humble and gentle; be patient, bearing with one another in love. Make every effort to keep the unity of the Spirit through the bond of peace.

Galatians 1:10 – Am I now trying to win the approval of human beings, or of God? Or am I trying to please people? If I were still trying to please people, I would not be a servant of Christ.

Matthew 6:1 – "Be careful not to practice your righteousness in front of others to be seen by them. If you do, you will have no reward from your Father in heaven.

Philippians 2:4 – Not looking to your own interests but each of you to the interests of the others.

Psalm 100:2 – Worship the LORD with gladness; come before him with joyful songs.

Romans 12:1 – Therefore, I urge you, brothers and sisters, in view of God's mercy, to offer your bodies as a living sacrifice, holy and pleasing to God--this is your true and proper worship.

Strength
2 Chronicles 20:12 – Our God, will you not judge them? For we have no power to face this vast army that is attacking us. We do not know what to do, but our eyes are on you."

Habakkuk 3:19 – The Sovereign LORD is my strength; he makes my feet like the feet of a deer, he enables me to tread on the heights. For the director of music. On my stringed instruments.

Judges 16:28 – Then Samson prayed to the LORD, "Sovereign LORD, remember me. Please, God, strengthen me just once more, and let me with one blow get revenge on the Philistines for my two eyes."

Nehemiah 8:10 NLT – And Nehemiah continued, "Go and celebrate with a feast of rich foods and sweet drinks, and share gifts of food with people who have nothing prepared. This is a sacred day before our Lord. Don't be dejected and sad, for the joy of the LORD is your strength!"

Philippians 4:13 – I can do all this through him who gives me strength.

Psalm 46:1 – For the director of music. Of the Sons of Korah. According to alamoth. A song. God is our refuge and strength, an ever-present help in trouble.

Psalm 73:26-28 – Those who are far from you will perish; you destroy all who are unfaithful to you. But as for me, it is good to be near God. I have made the Sovereign LORD my refuge; I will tell of all your deeds.

Ten Commandments
Exodus 20 –
Thou shall have no other Gods before me
Thou shall not worship idols for I am the Lord your God
Thou shall not take the name of the Lord your God in vain
Remember the Sabbath day to keep it holy
Honor your father and your mother
Thou shall not kill
Thou shall not commit adultery
Thou shall not steal
Thou shall not bear false witness against your neighbor
Thou shall not covert your neighbor

Thanksgiving

1 Thessalonians 5:18-19 – Give thanks in all circumstances; for this is God's will for you in Christ Jesus. Do not quench the Spirit.

Psalm 100:4 – Enter his gates with thanksgiving and his courts with praise; give thanks to him and praise his name.

Psalm 118:24 – The LORD has done it this very day; let us rejoice today and be glad.

Truthfulness

Luke 12:2 – There is nothing concealed that will not be disclosed, or hidden that will not be made known.

Trust in Him

Isaiah 26:4 – Trust in the LORD forever, for the LORD, the LORD himself, is the Rock eternal.

Proverbs 28:25-26 – The greedy stir up conflict, but those who trust in the LORD will prosper. Those who trust in themselves are fools, but those who walk in wisdom are kept safe.

Proverbs 29:25 – Fear of man will prove to be a snare, but whoever trusts in the LORD is kept safe.

Psalm 5:3 – In the morning, LORD, you hear my voice; in the morning I lay my requests before you and wait expectantly.

Psalm 7:1 ESV – O LORD my God, in you do I take refuge; save me from all my pursuers and deliver me,

Psalm 9:10 – Those who know your name trust in you, for you, LORD, have never forsaken those who seek you.

Psalm 13:1-6 – Trust Prayer

For the director of music. A psalm of David. How long, LORD? Will you forget me forever? How long will you hide your face from me? How long must I wrestle with my thoughts and day after day have sorrow in my heart? How long will my enemy triumph over me?

Look on me and answer, LORD my God. Give light to my eyes, or I will sleep in death,

and my enemy will say, "I have overcome him," and my foes will rejoice when I fall.

But I trust in your unfailing love; my heart rejoices in your salvation. I will sing the LORD's praise, for he has been good to me.

Psalm 28:7 – The LORD is my strength and my shield; my heart trusts in him, and he helps me. My heart leaps for joy, and with my song I praise him.

Psalm 37:4 – Take delight in the LORD, and he will give you the desires of your heart.

Psalm 57:1 – For the director of music. To the tune of "Do Not Destroy." Of David. A miktam. When he had fled from Saul into the cave. Have mercy on me, my God, have mercy on me, for in you I take refuge. I will take refuge in the shadow of your wings until the disaster has passed.

Psalm 86:2 – Guard my life, for I am faithful to you; save your servant who trusts in you. You are my God.

Psalm 91:2 - I will say of the LORD, "He is my refuge and my fortress, my God, in whom I trust."

Psalm 143:8-9 – Let the morning bring me word of your unfailing love, for I have put my trust in you. Show me the way I should go, for to you I entrust my life. Rescue me from my enemies, LORD, for I hide myself in you.

Psalm 147:11 – The LORD delights in those who fear him, who put their hope in his unfailing love.

Water (Living)
John 7:37-38 – On the last and greatest day of the festival, Jesus stood and said in a loud voice, "Let anyone who is thirsty come to me and drink. Whoever believes in me, as Scripture has said, rivers of living water will flow from within them."

Weakness
1 Corinthians 1:27 NIV – God chose the weak things of the world to shame the strong.

2 Corinthians 12:9 AMP – But He has said to me, "My grace is sufficient for you: for power is being perfected in weakness.

Wisdom
Colossians 3:16 - Let the message of Christ dwell among you richly as you teach and admonish one another with all wisdom through psalms, hymns, and songs from the Spirit, singing to God with gratitude in your hearts.

James 1:5 – If any of you lacks wisdom, you should ask God, who gives generously to all without finding fault, and it will be given to you.

Proverbs 16:1 - To humans belong the plans of the heart, but from the LORD comes the proper answer of the tongue.

Worship God
Proverbs 28:14 – Blessed is the one who always trembles before God, but whoever hardens their heart falls into trouble.

Sofia Grace is the eldest of three siblings. With her parents, brother, and sister, they migrated to the United States at a very young age and have lived there ever since. She has been married for 32 years and blessed with two beautiful and now grown-up children.

Sofia wants to share how she fell to the lowest and most depressing point of her life only to be spiritually raised up by the Almighty God. "I tried to commit suicide three times and God spoke to me and said, "Your life is not ending, it is just about to begin."" At the age of 50, Sofia's new life began just as God had promised.

As a first-time author, Sofia admittedly shared her weakness in writing, but God placed it in her heart to write a book and she obeyed. Just as her name means "strength and wisdom come from God", Sofia devoted her study time to write and prayed daily for strength and wisdom to complete her first book.

"And He said to me, "My grace is sufficient for you, for My strength is made perfect in weakness." (2 Corinthians 12:9a NKJV).

I pray that my testimony and/or testimony shared by others in this book will help you or someone you may know who may be falling and may need the Holy Spirit to raise you up. If I can help one person just by reading my book, then I have done what God has asked me to do. May God's strength and wisdom be with you always.

Please visit the Sofia Grace Ministry at https://liveinfaitheveryday.org/

Printed in the United States
By Bookmasters